To

been the same w/...
independent spirit. Your presence
was a blessing to me on this
journey. God bless you, Amanda!

Patrick Both

DEDICATION

The journey is dedicated to the donors who made it possible.

The stories are dedicated to the Racers I called family for 2015.

The lessons learned are dedicated to the missionaries who hosted us during our journey and continue to bring Kingdom to the world.

ISBN: 1523901438
ISBN-13: 978-1523901432

All rights reserved.

Copyright © 2015 Patrick Booth

The Long Road Home

Lived, Witnessed and Shared By:
Patrick Booth

Edited By:
Britney Cossey

Who I am:
My name is Patrick Booth. I am a young man who has spent most of my life's years in a quiet little suburb north of Dallas, Texas. I have been blessed in countless ways throughout my lifetime, for which I will be ever grateful. I am a son, grandson, uncle, brother, counselor, critic, entrepreneur, leader, follower, lover, and hater.

What I've done, where I've been:
I have always been called to help people. I was blessed to receive hardship in my youth so that I would be prepared to deal with it as an adult. I never went through that hardship without love and support from my family, friends, and church family, though. This has always driven me to try to give back blessings as much as I receive them. This calling has pushed me to dedicate my life to counseling others through their difficulties, volunteering routinely with local charities, and traveling with church groups to places as far as South Africa, Mozambique, Chile, Guatemala, Costa Rica, and Mexico.

What and where I am called to go and do:
I now hear a changing in the wind. In the past, I have sought to satisfy my need to help others through a career in counseling. This has been very challenging, but equally indescribably rewarding. My commitment to this limited my opportunities to travel abroad and spread the love I long to share in more expansive ways. This is no longer the case. I am making a commitment to immerse myself in the cultures where my love can help the most. This book is about my experiences in Colombia, Chile, Argentina, Peru, Bolivia, Panama, Costa Rica*, Nicaragua, Guatemala, El Salvador, and Honduras.

Along with the World Race project by Adventures in Missions, I was able to spend a full month in each of these countries in 2015 spreading love, compassion, and understanding to those I met along my journey.

Thank you so much to all of you who have shown me support in the past and whose spirits will continue to boost mine as I journey to provide compassion to a world longing for love.

*The route was changed to include Colombia, Chile and Argentina instead of Puerto Rico, the Dominican Republic, and Costa Rica. Despite this, our squad would stop for a weeklong debrief in Costa Rica along the new route.

CONTENTS

PROLOGUE 1

PREPARING FOR THE JOURNEY 5
- Let's Get This Started 6
- Training Camp 8
- Team Tear #1 – Ryan 20
- Letting Go of Preparation 21
- Atlanta Today, El Salvador Tomorrow 23

EL SALVADOR 25
- Summary 26
- Service 29
- Team Tear #2 – Allison 31
- Angeles Y Maria 33
- When Dreaming Ends 36
- Unexpected Greeting 38
- Team Tear #3 – Jeff 39
- Team Tear #4 – Katrina 41
- Favorite Moments 43

GUATEMALA 45
- Summary 46
- Service 48
- Claire's Healing 50
- Healing a Wounded Heart 51
- Unexpected Greeting 54
- Forget the World Race 55
- Betsy's Coat 60
- Favorite Moments 63

HONDURAS 65
- Summary 66
- Service 68
- Team Tear #5 – Leah 70
- Juan Carlos 71

ASHLEY'S THROAT	74
UNEXPECTED GREETING	75
FAVORITE MOMENTS	76

NICARAGUA 77

SUMMARY	78
GRANADA	80
LEARNING FORGIVENESS	82
JENNYFER	85
LYDIETTE	86
TOM	87
UNEXPECTED GREETING	90
SARA	91
FAVORITE MOMENTS	93

COSTA RICA 95

SUMMARY	96
TREASURE HUNTING	97
TEAM TEAR #6 – BRENNA	103
TEAM TEAR #7 – RYAN	104
FAVORITE MOMENTS	105

PANAMA 107

SUMMARY	108
SERVICE	110
UNEXPECTED GREETING	114
LEADERSHIP DEVELOPMENT WORKSHOP	115
FAVORITE MOMENTS	116

COLOMBIA 117

SUMMARY	118
SERVICE	120
RICHARD*	122
WHAT PICTURES COULD NEVER SHOW	124
UNEXPECTED GREETING	127
JAMIE*	128

TEAM TEAR #8 – JUSTIN	129
TEAM TEAR #9 – AMANDA	130
LUKE*	132
FAVORITE MOMENTS	135

ECUADOR 137
SUMMARY	138
PARENT VISION TRIP	139
SERVICE	140
BEING JESUS	142
UNEXPECTED GREETING	145
FAVORITE MOMENTS	146

PERU 149
SUMMARY	150
SERVICE	152
OPENING DOORS	156
UNEXPECTED GREETING	158
FAVORITE MOMENTS	159

BOLIVIA 161
SUMMARY	162
SERVICE	167
I AM GOING HOME	168
MORE THAN PITY	170
UNEXPECTED GREETING	172
FAVORITE MOMENTS	173

CHILE 175
SUMMARY	176
SERVICE	179
UNEXPECTED GREETING	183
FAVORITE MOMENTS	184

ARGENTINA 185
SUMMARY & SERVICE	186
THIS IS NOT THE END	196

UNEXPECTED GREETING	198
THREE BEDS	199
THE LONG ROAD HOME	200
FAVORITE MOMENTS	201
EPILOGUE	202
WORLD RACE CONTACTS	207

Prologue
Fear

This morning I woke in my bed a little before dawn. I could not rest. The reason was not a mystery to me. Yesterday afternoon I had a conversation with my business partner about selling my portion of the business. She described her family confronting her about selling the business. They warned that she could not find work in the industry within the metroplex any longer. I knew going into the business three years ago that this would be the case for me as well. Nevertheless, we had embarked down this road together and it had paid off well for us.

Now I face the decision of leaving this road behind me. Along with it, I'm leaving behind the experience and education I have built for the last ten years of my life. The knowledge from these experiences will always be with me, but it is specifically suited for the industry I have been engrossed in. A new opportunity means truly starting a brand-new life.

It is dark.

I walk out of my apartment to face faint light from the hint of a promised sunrise. I'm wearing my robe and sandals, as it is a cold morning today. I begin to walk toward the faint light, but looking around me I see a star in the opposite direction behind me. I walk toward the star, asking God for guidance and understanding. As I round the building of my apartment, I see a full moon lighting up the darkness in the sky. I continue to walk towards it, thanking God for the countless blessings in my life and asking for His wisdom to guide me. It draws me to the opposite edge of my apartment building, so I turn and face the original direction.

The sunlight is a little brighter.

I walk towards it. As I walk, I begin to reach the far edge of the apartment complex. The pavement turns to clean-cut grass and just beyond this lies an open field, completely uncared for. My behavior mimics my feelings. I walk without hesitation into the clear-cut grass, but stop at the edge of the wild field. The clear-cut grass represents my business. Although it is off the beaten pavement, it is still groomed and tailored to the life that I had been working towards. Leaving my business behind me would mean walking into the wild field. Walking into a territory that has no use and no concern for the experiences I have had in the past.

The sunlight has now illuminated the clouds.

Walking to the divider between the grass and the field, I see between the clouds a star. It is a single star that can still be seen with the dawning light. I pray for God's wisdom in the day just as he provides me rest in the night. I let the prayer resonate as I begin to walk along the division between the grass and the field.

The clear-cut grass leads me to a road. I begin to cross it and recognize the source of my fear. Selling my business means I will never be a counselor in the industry or area I have always worked before. It is a different kind of fear than I have known at other times in my life. When I started my business at twenty-eight years old, many people praised me for being courageous. I was simply prepared to fail. I had thought at that point, "If the business does not succeed and I cannot find work any longer, I will simply see that God has other plans for my life." Now, I am thirty-one years old and am considering giving away what I have built, in order to pursue what I originally thought of as Plan B. Crossing this road means that I cannot come back across it.

The dawn is hindered as clouds cover its light.

I walk across the road, again asking for God's wisdom as I consider this decision. Across the road is a pond. I follow this pond to a stream pouring out of it. There is a concrete bank on either side of this stream. I sit and ponder the countless thoughts pulling me in infinite directions. As the sun rises, I consider walking across the creek. I roll up my pajama pant legs and take off my sandals. I see that the concrete on each side is stable, solid. It is where I am standing now. There is stable, solid ground on the other side, but I must cross the creek in order to reach it. I step into the water to find it is deeper than I thought and much more slippery. Change is more difficult than most would imagine it to be. I find my footing nonetheless. I must stabilize myself in the slippery, shallow water so that I can place a foot on the firm ground of the outside bank. As I bring both feet onto secure footing, I turn to see the path I have trod. Although the apartment is only across the street, it feels very far away.

Sunlight is breaking through the clouds.

I begin to see the minute journey that I have taken this morning as an analogy for the turning point faced in my life. I see all at once the star guiding me in the night, the moon providing respite in the darkness, the sunlight drawing me out toward the wild field, the road that must be crossed, and the creek providing a challenge between two sides of stability. I step back into the creek and become comfortable with the water rushing over my feet, soothing my skin. I become comfortable with change and with the challenges change will always bring with it. I know that God provides me stability on either side. What a wonderful blessing it is to have to choose between two good things.

The dawn is clear and sunlight fills the sky

Preparing for the Journey

Let's Get This Started

This vision is becoming more and more clear with each passing day. What once seemed like an impractical dream is quickly becoming a very immediate reality. People close to me have spoken words of encouragement:
"I believe in you."
"You're goin' to do good for the whole world."
"You have such a wonderful heart; I want you to go and be successful."
"You're gonna do so many amazing things for so many people."
But as I hear these kind words, I am beginning to come to another realization about the World Race altogether: I must live up to it.

The World Race is not a mission trip. It is not a spiritual exploration. It is an incredible testament of faith. It is innumerable people expressing trust with their donations. It is a chorus of vocalists harmonizing to sound a song of pleasant comfort to those who are suffering. It is a marathon of runners who gather for one unified purpose: **to show love to the world, no matter the distance that must be reached.**

The foundation of the World Race is in the group of faceless participants who never see another country. Its spirit lives in the prayers and support from everyone at home. Its strength is embodied by coaches who empower volunteers to go beyond their comfort zone. Those of us standing at the starting line, we are just lucky enough to be its body.

So, I make a solemn pledge. I will not accept donations for a personal vacation. I will not accept prayers for my individual wellbeing.

I will forget myself. I will lose myself. I will become a simple conduit that transmits these generous offerings to where they need to be: to the communities who need construction, to the lives who need healing, to the hearts who need comfort, and to the souls longing for peace.

Let's get this thing started!

This journey is yours and I long to share it with you.

Training Camp

Application

My relationship with Adventures in Missions began through an extensive application process they do fully online, with the exception of a final phone interview. They begin with a background check, then ask for brief descriptions of faith, then have questionnaires about medical history and personal challenges (including things such as criminal history, violence, family abuse, suicidal ideation, etc.). After these are completed, they invite you to participate in the interview. This is also online and is a short answer questionnaire about everything from family history, to your faith, to explanations about the previous questionnaire. After all of this process, they get to the phone interview, which is generally just to confirm the answers you gave online and tell you of your approval.

It's a pretty extensive process, which I was pleased about because I assumed it meant they're keeping everyone on the team safe.

Fundraising

After going through this arduous process, you are given a time frame of a couple weeks to submit a deposit of $250 in order to claim your spot on the team. Then, the fund-raising begins. They give you a bunch of resource links and some generic online training, but pretty much leave it to you to get your funds. There are deadlines you have to meet, but they're all pretty reasonable. About 25% by training camp, 25% more before you launch, 25% more a few months in, then the full amount about halfway through your trip.

They do setup the blog and an account to receive tax-deductible-donations for you, which is very helpful.

Communication

They immediately sign you up for their team blog and team Facebook group. They do most of their communication on the team blog, but the word spreads more easily on the Facebook group. There is also a mobilizer that keeps in touch with you occasionally on the phone.

Pre-training Camp

They gave men a Man-Hike option and women a Beauty for Ashes option, both free three-day retreats prior to seven-day training camp. My first day was cut short because I missed my flight and was delayed for six hours. I was very concerned, but put to ease by the mobilizer who called me back after I left her a voicemail. She gave me the leader of the Man-Hike's number and when I got in touch with him he said that they would send a bus to the airport later if enough people were delayed. Luckily, this is what happened.

The Man-Hike consisted of two days straight hiking, from the morning till late afternoon. It was 9 miles on day one and 12 miles on day two. We had a guy pass out on day two, which delayed the hike for an hour and half while an ambulance was called to come pick him up on the trail at a service road. The rest of us went on to finish the trail after that.

In my opinion, the Man-Hike was done well. They did a very brief devotional on night one, then a quick debrief on day two. They seemed to allow the experience itself to be everything it needed to be and it did provide a bonding experience for the men doing it. From what was told to me, the Beauty for Ashes retreat was a great bonding experience that consisted mainly of comfortably confiding in one another and exploring personal growth.

Training Camp

The first day of training camp set the stage for the rest of the week. Two other men on my squad had gone on the Man-Hike, so we got to know each other early. The organization asked us to leave the property while they prepared everything for camp, so we had some time to kill before registration. We decided to go into town and shower up at the YMCA. We joked that we should come back pampered in bathrobes, with cigars and loafers. At Wal-Mart we found bathrobes that matched our squad colors, so we each got one and wore them to registration. I kept mine on for the rest of the week!

Photo courtesy: Carlie Smith

After registration, they herded us to our respective campgrounds where we setup tents and began to introduce ourselves. One of the first things they talked about when we returned for our lecture was letting go of past resentments. They then let us take an hour to reflect on this. After that, they broke us into groups to discuss what we were comfortable sharing. This was an excellent exercise. It was timed well and the execution of it gave us our first time to really dig a little deeper getting to know one another. That night, they prayed over everyone at worship to let go of these grievances and there were a lot of tears flowing. I mostly put my arm around a few people and prayed with them as they let go.

Closing the night, they introduced us to the concept that each morning we were going to have a team exercise. They asked for a volunteer from each squad and nobody seemed anxious to jump up there. So I did. The guy speaking handed each of us an envelope and proceeded to tell us that tomorrow morning we were supposed to read the instructions to our squad. Since I was only half listening, I immediately opened the envelope that was handed to me and started reading it. As I did this, I noticed the speaker stopped. I looked up to see everyone staring at me and I turned to the speaker to see him staring at me disapprovingly. I shrugged my shoulders and started putting the paper back into the envelope. He proceeded to say that these would be read tomorrow morning.

A few of my squad mates said they loved that action because they felt it greatly represented our squad's attitude.

The next morning, the instruction said to pack up everything and hike for half an hour. It was repeated again the next morning, except that we ran for half an hour instead of hiking. Another morning, we took a short walk focusing on how our packs felt and they gave us some pointers on making the packs more comfortable by balancing the weight. These were the most basic exercises we did. Role-playing exercises were used throughout the week also.

One time we had to partner up, and then choose one person to be a lion and one a giraffe. After we chose, they told us the giraffes had lost their luggage and could not have it for the next 24 hours. Another night, they told us we'd be stuck in the airport. That night we slept in a warehouse style room with the lights on all night and airport sounds blasting through loud speakers. One night we were told we would have to leave our packs at campsite and make a group camping night out of tarps and a little rope.

The backpacking pointers were helpful to make things more comfortable. The time they told us we could not use our packs was helpful to remind us to rely on/support each other. The airport exercise was not very helpful, other than teaching us to deal with discomfort. The camping night was a great bonding experience because we created our own entertainment and pallets to sleep on. However, during the camping exercise they arbitrarily selected leaders beforehand that clearly were not comfortable in the role. They were quickly aided by a couple boy scouts, who helped set up the campground, and a few social girls helped set up some group games.

They spent two days doing small group team-building exercises with us. Individually, they asked us afterward who we liked to work with, didn't like to work with, who else we would like to work with, etc. Our teams were switched each time. The second day, after doing one in the morning, we were asked to give a thumbs-up, thumbs-down, or thumb-in-the-middle about how we felt about this being our team for all year. We were then reminded that we would need to be able to challenge each other's growth, as well as support one another. They began to give us examples of support by asking what we each liked about three of the people in the group. At that point, they said we were done and had free time. We quickly asked what about the other four people in the group. It was explained that it was just for example's sake. We took our free time to continue the process of going around the circle, then saying what we liked about each person in the group with us. We each prayed around the circle to close out, as I closed by praying over each of my teammates by name. A few hours later, they told us our teams had been selected and it was that same team. They asked us to do the exercise, which we quickly said we had already done. Our squad leader then asked to just pray over us and he prayed over each of us by name as well. We were then given about six hours to spend together for free time. It was the only time we were allowed to leave the property to go into town.

Their team selection was a great process. It was wonderful that they asked each individual privately who they preferred and did not prefer. It was also excellent that they gave us the opportunity to deny the team. Although it seemed an uncomfortable question, I am glad they did it openly because it encourages direct communication. In fact, two of our people put their thumbs in the middle. When I spoke about why I had put my thumb up, I said the group seemed to be very intentional and was hesitant because we had built relationships with our whole squad. It felt like breaking the other relationships a little to commit to this particular team. The other two members agreed and moved their thumbs up. Conversation is a wonderful thing! I was surprised when they did not allow us to go around the whole circle encouraging one another, but I suppose that's probably because they sometimes have to change the group afterward. The free time they gave us is a phenomenal practice. It allowed us to get to know each other better than we had throughout the whole week and gave shape to the bonds we will need to start the journey together.

Team selection had occurred on Thursday. The following day was the only day dedicated to practical information. This is the day that they told us our launch date, launch process, how family can be involved and communicated with, and information about blogging. They also included talks about follow-up programs that they encourage people to do after the World Race. Then, they told us that we had to arrange our own transportation to the airport the following morning. Saturday morning each squad was given assignments and the participants cleaned up the property before parting ways.

A few of the best activities that they planned were a lake swim and mock foreign market:

1) One afternoon, they separated the men and women. They did not tell us what we were doing. We were loaded onto a bus and driven to a lakeside home. We were walked out back and told to take a log. Then we were walked to the lake and told to take the log, without getting it wet, across the lake to some men on the other side. They were handheld logs, but the lake still looked pretty wide. When I said they were joking they assured me they were not and told us we had thirty seconds to get into the water. I took off my bathrobe and walked in. The water was cold. By about a quarter of the way across, I could not touch bottom anymore. I turned to see one of my squad mates nearby. He seemed to be doing fine, but complained that he could not make it. I told him he was doing all right. He continued to complain; I continued to encourage. I began swimming backwards and just kept getting him to swim to me. Slowly, we made progress to about halfway across the lake. He said it just couldn't be done and began to say he would drown. I told him let's swim to the side bank, take a little break, then we'd keep going forward. He tossed his log and began swimming ardently for the side bank. I picked up his log and followed after him. We walked for a little bit along the bank before it broke to the right. We would have to swim the rest of the way across. He had renewed his strength and we made this last quarter of the lake easily. (Another teammate of mine had given up when he lost his footing. However, we had a guy who used to be a competitive swimmer on our team also. He went back and pulled the first guy across the lake. Both floating on their backs, with one kicking and dragging the other.)

It was a good experience for a few reasons. It showed us that even when something looks impossible, it can be done. It reminded us of our own limitations, since almost all of us had to get our logs wet before making it to the other side. It gave us an opportunity to encourage and rely on one another.

2) The mock market experience was a lot of fun! One night, they told us we would be buying our own food. We were given some money and broken up into teams of five each. There was a market setup on campgrounds meant to simulate a crowded foreign market in other countries. They warned us that whatever we bought would be our only dinner and that there may be pickpockets or thieves in the market. My team consisted of four girls and me. Immediately, they strapped their backpacks to their chests rather than their backs. I suggested we move as a unit closely together. They all agreed. I also suggested we look over the market before buying anything. (This proved to be a mistake because it took up too much time.)

We pushed our way through the crowded market street. I literally walked beside the girls making sure I was within arm's reach of all of them at the same time. The setup was just one street with booths on both sides that strung about 25 yards in length. We made it to one side and then had to work our way back to the beginning because the only currency exchange was at the first table coming in. This ate up a lot of our time. We made it through and back with no problems. As we approached the currency exchange table, a woman with a sleeveless throw nudged her way into our circle. I immediately pushed her out of the circle to avoid her pickpocketing any of us.

A man came up and said, "Hey, hey, man. Do you see that girl?"

I said, "Yeah. Yeah, she's a good looking girl, isn't she?" This made me chuckle and one of my teammates laugh. He admonished me not to touch her. I said all right and he moved along.

As we began speaking with the moneychanger, another man came walking up near my group. As he began to nudge his way in, I put my elbow into his chest and pushed him out. He gave me a look of questioning distress and in broken English said, "Hey, hey, my friend?"

As if he could not speak the words, "Why would you push me?"

I answered with a calm soothing voice, "Yeah, yeah, my friend, my friend." Asserting my spot physically between him and the girls in my group, but signifying that I meant him no personal harm.

He stayed there in the crowd while one of the girls exchanged her money, but he could not get any closer because I stood between him and the four girls. After she exchanged the money, he walked off. I was still wearing my bathrobe. He subtly pulled on my bathrobe pocket with a few fingers as he squeezed his way out of the crowded group of people.

I laughed to myself as I let him do it. "What do you think you are likely to pickpocket from a guy wearing a bathrobe to the market?" There was nothing in my pocket for him to steal.

A bus came rolling through and I reached out to make sure that the girls in my group were not in its way. Another girl from our squad, but not on my team for this exercise was nearby and I instinctively shoved her out of the way also. She thought it was funny and we joked later that she was already out of harm's way, but thanked me for my concern anyway.

We pushed our way back through the market without incident. I felt a tug on my bathrobe belt once, but it was double-knotted so it didn't go anywhere. We exited the market with plates of fish. We began to eat them and noticed another team sitting away from the market. I wondered if they had not gotten anything to eat. We walked over and they had food. They were just waiting on a final member to come out with the last plate they were buying. Because we did not have exact change, we had a little extra fish. I offered it to them for the price we paid. They bought it from us.

We went back into the market after we'd each finished our fish. To avoid the heavy crowd, we walked around the backside of the market. I laughed as we entered to see a stand setup of stuff that had been stolen from people during the exercise! I pointed it out to my teammates. The shopkeeper quickly corrected me by saying these were "recycled" goods. I said "Sure, whatever."

He struck up a conversation about coming from America himself and asked about why we were there. We talked for a minute as we passed by his shop. I had some money in my hand as we were walking away, but had folded it over to be sure of a strong grip. I was glad that I did! Before I noticed, while I was walking away, he reached over the crowd to try to grab the cash from my hand. He pulled, but it did not move as his fingers slipped off. I turned and chided him, laughing that he had tried but could not take it.

Shops started closing and we realized that we were on a limited time. We approached a shop that had a beggar outside of it. I knew we would not spend all of the money we had left because this was the last shop open. I reached down to give him some money. He took it gracefully and placed it under the plate of food someone else must have given him. While we were waiting, he began to wail. I turned and one of my teammates embarrassingly told me she had accidentally kicked over his plate of food. I looked around and there were no immediate threats, so I knelt down and placed his food back onto his plate. He immediately stopped wailing. We were still waiting to make our purchase and I joked that he was going to eat better than we were. He lowered his head and raised his food up for us to take it. I was amazed! I denied it though and told him I was just joking.

As the shops closed, the crowd cleared away, the beggar left, and my team was the last to make their purchase. Each of the ladies went first, and then we began walking to our next destination. As I picked up the last plate, a hand reached over my shoulder and snatched a bite from my plate.

I turned to face someone in sunglasses and a bandana saying, "You weren't gonna eat that, were you?"

I glanced over him for a brief second, then reached quickly into his shirt pocket and pulled out a PowerBar. I put it into my pocket and stood there waiting for him to react. He paused for a moment, and then began to walk off. He eyed me as he walked away, saying, "Okay. You win this time, my friend. You win this time." I smiled and joined the rest of my team at our base camp with my plate of food.

When they did the follow-up conversation they asked us how the experience was and gave us some pointers to keep ourselves safe from thieves and pickpockets in crowded areas. When I told the group I stole from the thief, the squad leader who was leading the discussion turned and just started laughing. I don't think she knew how to respond. As I explained what I had done, I pulled the PowerBar out and offered it first to my team before eating some of it myself. It tasted like sweet victory and it felt good to see that on the faces of my team members.

All in all, I feel like I got a great experience out of this exercise: I flipped the market by reselling food I'd bought to other Americans, I was offered charity from a beggar, none of my teammates experienced any hardships or loss, and I stole from a thief. It was a good day.

The best experiences were private moments with other campers. Examples were letting a guy who did not know how to swim know how proud of him and what an inspiration he was when we all swam across the lake. Another example was speaking with the man that passed out on the Man-Hike, letting him know that he inspired us because he pushed himself harder than the rest of us.

The best moments with my actual squad were between activities planned on the schedule. Between lunch and our next talk, we all were sitting around the lunch tables after everyone else left. Everyone was talking and learning each other's backgrounds when a girl mentioned she majored in opera singing. She sang for us and everyone fell silent in awe. Two other people sang a cappella. Each received an immediate applause from the whole squad. Two nights during the week, after all the planned events had concluded, our squad met to discuss our expectations of each other and throughout the race. Being a counselor, it was my pleasure to verbally lead the first one and then begin the second one. (By the second one, the group was comfortable enough with each other to just speak very freely.)

These were not scheduled; they were simply something our squad decided to do together. They were the best and most unifying experiences our squad shared together during the week.

Team Tear #1 – Ryan

During training camp, one of the first lectures they gave was one about taking an inventory of losses. They told us to identify past hurts in our lives, so they would not catch us off guard on the race. They then gave us an hour to do this before having a small group discussion with the men on our squad. Ryan and Jeff both spoke of being cheated on by their girlfriends, but Ryan specified that his girlfriend cheated on him with his best friend. He also admitted with shame that he had cheated on his next girlfriend. I spoke last in the discussion and related my personal experiences to each of the other men's significant losses. This was particularly easy to emphasize with the two guys who had been cheated on.

That evening, during worship, they prayed over everyone to be free from their past hurts. They prayed for everyone to be free from the identities they had established in sin, like slut, cheater, or tramp. Ryan was standing near me and slumped down in his chair. He put his hands over his face and wept. I walked over to him and knelt down to put my arm around him. I prayed for him. Wiping his eyes, he stood up and embraced me in a strong hug. He sat back down afterward and continued to pray. As I stood nearby, I was happy to see a few others come up and speak life over him.

Letting Go of Preparation

How do we prepare for a journey that will change us forever? What can we bring with us on a path that will refute everything we once were?

There is no way to describe the vast experiences shared during the ten days we met the squad we'll be traveling with for the next year. There were outpourings of tears, constant laughter, boisterous worship, and even some occasional quiet reflection. Bonds were formed through shared suffering, personal support, intimate vulnerability, and individual strengths. A family was formed that will see its members through thick and thin, in ways none of us can imagine until it happens.

Since I know many of my supporters are curious as to my own personal experience, I'll try to summarize it as best I can: I hiked twenty miles in the first two days, stopping to drink water directly out of three different streams. I lived in a bathrobe for the remainder of the training camp. I enjoyed meeting an eclectic group of people and seeing how our *very different* life paths had led us to this crossing. I tried my best to stay awake during many of the organization's informational talks. (Okay, so I didn't really try my best, but I did stay awake through most of them anyway.) I got to know my own strengths and weaknesses through various team-building exercises. I thoroughly enjoyed seeing team members' strengths blossom during particular exercises. I was reintroduced to my disgust for what a friend calls "rock-star worship music."

<u>I was challenged to let go of the limitations I put on my faith.</u>

This last challenge is certainly the answer to what we bring with us. For many of us, our whole lives have been a constant attempt to create a life for ourselves. We create an inner circle of family and friends that comfort us. We strive for a career to fulfill our need for accomplishment. We develop a lifestyle that we can use to identify who we are, but as each of these areas of our lives become full, we lose space for what else could be. Faith is said to be the belief in what we cannot see. But, as our horizon is filled with our own ambitions, we begin to believe what we see is all that there is. We forget that the world beyond our understanding is so much greater than we can imagine.

I will prepare for this journey by forgetting myself. I will bring with me acceptance. I will leave my self-imposed limitations behind.

I invite you to take this journey with me. I invite you to ask yourself what limitations you have put on your own understanding, on your own faith, and on your own life. I invite you to let these limitations go.

Atlanta Today, El Salvador Tomorrow

This is the last night I will spend in America for 11 months.

We've been in a hotel in Atlanta for three days. We've all heard far too many "inspirational talks." We're biting at the bit to start the path before us.

Despite our frustration, it will be hard to say goodbye to three-quarters of our squad tomorrow as each team goes their separate ways. This realization brings to light how much will be missed throughout the year.

I am sorry for the lives I will miss while I am away. I am sorry for the weddings I cannot celebrate and the new babies I cannot greet. I am sorry for those who know I love them, but will not be able to hear it from me directly.

Thank you to all of you who have donated to this path. By your donation, you have made your own sacrifice and have also chosen to share love with the world.

I can only promise to honor your donations by sharing love, always.

Tonight Everything Changes

PATRICK BOOTH

El Salvador

Summary

Our first month together was certainly a transition period for all of us. There were many experiences that we shared which seemed to be indicative of how the rest of the race would look for us. However, many of these experiences were unique to El Salvador:

- <u>We slept, ate, worked, and played in the same three open rooms together all the time.</u> Warned and prepared for living in community, we thought this was fairly normal. Surprisingly, though, none of our other teams spent as much time together we did during the first month. It brought us together, but was also exhausting as we were still getting to know each other.

- <u>We had access to Internet 24/7.</u> This may seem like a trivial observation, but any world traveler will tell you finding access to the Internet and then discovering its cost can be quite cumbersome. This proved to be a double-edged sword for us. It allowed us to maintain contact with home, which helped lessen the impact of transitioning to new cultures (both El Salvador and the World Race have their own cultures). At the same time, it provided us a constant distraction from each other, which slowed our relationship development within our new team.

- <u>Our contact provided the best balance of ministry work, extra opportunities, and relaxation time I would ever experience on the race.</u> In that first month, we had a routine schedule, we were given optional opportunities to serve but were not pressured to maximize them, we were provided information about recreational excursions we could take, and we were granted the space to enjoy time by ourselves or with each other (some more). I am proud to say that our team often took the opportunities to invest more than was required in the community we were serving. The fact that this was our first month and we were all excited to serve certainly added to this, but I truly believe that our contact allowing us the space/time to recuperate each day contributed the most to a more full experience of family during our newfound journey.

- <u>We had team times/feedback every night.</u> The first night we were together, our squad leader, Greg introduced us to concepts called "team time" and "feedback". They're fairly self-explanatory: team time is time that is designated for the team to spend together in any way and feedback is a routine opportunity for team members to provide each other with positive affirmations and/or constructive criticism. Greg walked us through the process the first night and asked us to take turns leading the process throughout our time together. He said we would be having these times together each and every night. My teammate Jeff and I both laughed.

Greg didn't laugh. He was serious. Admittedly, I found this very redundant that first month. We slept, ate, worked, and played together all day, every day. We were almost never apart from one another. The idea of setting aside specific times each night to "share together" seemed wholly unnecessary. As we looked ahead at eleven months of daily, heart-wrenching, soul-searching conversations with people who we never spent time away from, the race suddenly seemed very heavy.

Despite our dread, this was the last month we had team time and feedback every night for varying reasons. Sometimes our ministry schedules simply wouldn't allow it nightly, sometimes teams just weren't interested and sometimes it just became more natural to allow feedback to flow organically when it arises. Later in the race, team times and feedback proved very important. Throughout the remainder of the race however, they would be used less or more depending on how often teams felt them to be necessary.

Service

Our service work this month consisted primarily of helping a child development center.

7:00 - 9:00 a.m.
We started each weekday by waking up and preparing breakfast for ourselves. Typically during this time, a few members of the team would be pulling all of our mattresses out of the classroom and stacking them into an office, out of the way for the rest of the day.

9:00 -10:00 a.m.
After breakfast, we would wash all of our dishes and prepare the center to receive the children. This consisted of sweeping every room, mopping every room, setting chair and tables up, then beginning to help the teachers who come in to prepare lunches for the children.

10:00 a.m. -12:30 p.m.
The children began arriving around 10:00-10:30 a.m. each day. We would then spend the next hour or so simply playing sports and games with them or doing puzzles with them. Some of the girls would be doing hair or letting the children do their hair. Boys would be wrestling or playing soccer. This was a time we could simply share joy in their lives.

12:30 - 1:30 p.m.
We would serve the children lunch. One of the children would pray while the group repeated their prayer, then we would take up their dishes and wash them. This proved to be quite the task since there were typically fifty to sixty children, along with the teachers and our team! The children would brush their teeth and take their vitamins at the end of lunch.

1:30 - 2:30 p.m.
This was the time dedicated to classwork. It would usually begin with a Bible lesson, followed by a reading/writing lesson, and end with a brief hands-on activity such as arts or crafts.

2:30 - 3:00 p.m.
The children would be gathered for one last snack time. Finger foods would be given, followed by a free time for play while the kids waited for their family members to come take them home.

The rest of the day would vary because it was our free time. Most days would involve us walking to the beach, which was five to ten minutes away by foot. At the beach, soccer was played regularly, giving us lots of opportunities to engage individuals in the community in a familiar, comfortable setting. Along with soccer, we enjoyed many swims in the ocean till day's end, routinely swimming out to jump the waves or let them crash into us. This was truly a simple, unexpected pleasure that made our first month very enjoyable.

Extra service projects this month included:
- *building and delivering beds for impoverished families*
- *helping with a church car wash*
- *participating in youth groups on Saturday evenings*
- *participating in worship services Sunday mornings*
- *maintaining a fish hatchery in a hydroponic system housed behind the child development center*
- *bringing a little life back to a dying garden in the hydroponic system*
- *performing a live skit on stage in the city square and then inviting viewers to visit the church.*

Team Tear #2 – Allison

Day two of month one is in El Salvador. We arrived on Saturday and participated in a youth group that evening. On Sunday, we went to church, had lunch with our contact, then most of the team slept for the better part of the afternoon while the squad leader, Greg, and I went to the beach with some of the youth.

He had demonstrated the night before that each night we would do team time and feedback. He had read a verse about dry bones, and then asked us what area of our life seemed to be dry and dead. Allison explained her sister and mom had not talked in 3 years. I shared that my sister had not talked with any of our family in 7 years. We prayed over one another and it was a good night. He also said it'd be easiest for our team to take turns leading these nights.

I volunteered to do Sunday. After thinking about what topic I thought was important, I decided to do a night focused on service. Our contact had been very gracious when discussing our projects, describing many as optional. He also said that it would be up to us to decide how much initiative we take.

So, for team time, I asked everyone to describe the greatest joyful experience they had serving others and how they would like to serve people over this next year. While they were talking, I pulled the mop bucket out of the shower and began to wash their feet. Leah, a teammate, was big into essential oils, so I was even able to douse oil on their feet after washing them. The look on everyone's face was priceless. The conversation stopped. I made a few jokes to keep it going. By the second pair of feet, Greg asked Allison what was going on. He had seen her begin to cry.

She said she had heard of this happening with other people, but had never experienced it. She also said her love language is serving others and she had found it difficult to expect other people to speak the same love language. Jeff asked her if she felt I was speaking her love language. She said yes. At that point it was her turn for her feet to be washed. As I washed her feet, my teammate Jeff said this was even cooler because I look like Jesus. I didn't have my beard or mustache.

This was a great experience. I had debated on washing one pair of feet, then passing it on. I decided at the last minute to do them all myself. I closed the night by saying I wanted to demonstrate that service is defined by action regardless of what kind of action it is. We need to be the team that takes the initiative. Every member of the team had a servant's heart and I told him or her as much. I encouraged them each to trust their spirit.

Angeles Y Maria

Today I am grateful for God's Spirit and influence in my life. A few days ago, my squad leader and I collided while playing soccer. This left me with a weak foot throughout the first few weeks of my trip. Because of that, he offered me a chance to share a devotional with some boys who I would normally be playing soccer with. I flipped through the Bible a little and opted to hand the option over to my teammate, Jeff. Jeff had seemed to be in a somber mood for the last few days, but he took the opportunity up without hesitation. He told me later that it was incredible because the words that he was sharing with these boys ended up being just the words he needed to hear himself.

While the others were playing soccer, I came inside to work with the younger children. A little girl, around the age of four, had been crying in the kitchen alone earlier in the day. As I came into the room, she was alone, sitting in a chair set aside for her, still crying. I began to walk to different tables and interact with the children as best I could. After a short while, I noticed she was now sitting at an activity table in the room by herself. She was still crying.

I sat down on the floor next to her little table. She had a paper where the children were instructed to draw the letter 'P'. I said *hola* and her sobbing slowed just a little. I asked her if she liked to write. She shook her head. I asked her if she could write. She said no. I repeated this dialogue for a few minutes, and then noticed the other papers. One was a picture of a potato. I asked her if she liked to draw. She said yes. I pulled the potato drawing out and put it on top. I asked her if she wanted to draw. She said yes and her sobbing stopped. She began to color the potato. I told her she drew well. She smiled.

When she finished, she pulled the next paper out. It was an outlined 'p'. She began to color that also. I told her she colored well. She smiled again. When these were finished, she held them up with pride. I told her to give them to her teacher. She ran up to the teacher with a smile. She came back and asked me to write her name on the pictures. I asked her if she could. She said no. I asked her name and she told me it was Angeles. I asked her to spell it out and she could not. I wrote her name on her papers.

We pulled out the writing paper with the p's on it. I asked her if she could write it. She said no. I asked her if I could help her. She said yes. I began to write p's on a few lines of her paper. I told her she could do it. She shook her head no. I slowly demonstrated the process of starting at the bottom, making a line up, and then making the circle. I put the pencil in her hand and she attempted to write a 'p'. It looked more like a 'D'. I told her good job!

Another little girl joined the table and demonstrated the 'p' a few times while saying, "*Tu puedes* (You can)." I encouraged the new girl, Maria, to help Angeles. Maria put the pencil in Angeles's hand and then explained the process in far better Spanish than I spoke! Angeles wrote her first 'p' and looked up with excited anticipation.

"*Muy bien!* (Very good!)" I exclaimed.

"*Y un otro* (And another)," I encouraged. She wrote another one and looked up with that same excited anticipation.

"*Tu escribes 'p'*, (You write 'p')," I told her.

She wrote another four more p's, looking up with excitement each time. At this time, the class was being put away. I thanked Maria for helping instruct Angeles and directed Angeles to take the paper to her teacher. She ran with excitement to show what she had done. When I saw her leave that day, she was jumping and playing. She was the last little girl to leave and she waved goodbye as she rode off in the back of her parents' truck. As far as my view stayed with her, she never stopped smiling.

THE LONG ROAD HOME

When Dreaming Ends

As I lie here awake, with my head resting on a child-size beanbag and the rest of my body resting on the tile floor below, I have time to reflect on the wonders of the past month. It has been such a blessing to be able to pour love into the children we've worked with: to play with them, to feed them, to encourage their learning, and to provide love in their lives. Each day, we would wake up and pack up our mattresses, since we slept in the room where the children learned each day.

Every day we would work with the children and occasionally we would support other projects as well. These ranged from building cement blocks for their driveway, helping the youth group with their car wash, putting together a mural for the church, playing soccer with locals and just sharing our ministry with the church who hosted us for the month. One final project was building bed frames for congregation members who lack beds for their children. As we completed this, the only thing lacking were mattresses to provide comfort while they slept.

Yesterday, I watched with joy as we gave away the beds we had built along with a couple extra mattresses we had... and the one I'd been sleeping on for the last three weeks. Then I saw the little boy climb into his new bed with a smile. We waved goodbye to the family as we left their two-room house that is the size of a typical American living room. The boys waved hurriedly and then rushed inside.

I will relish the opportunity that I have been blessed with: an opportunity to not only fulfill some children's dreams, but also provide space for them to dream more.

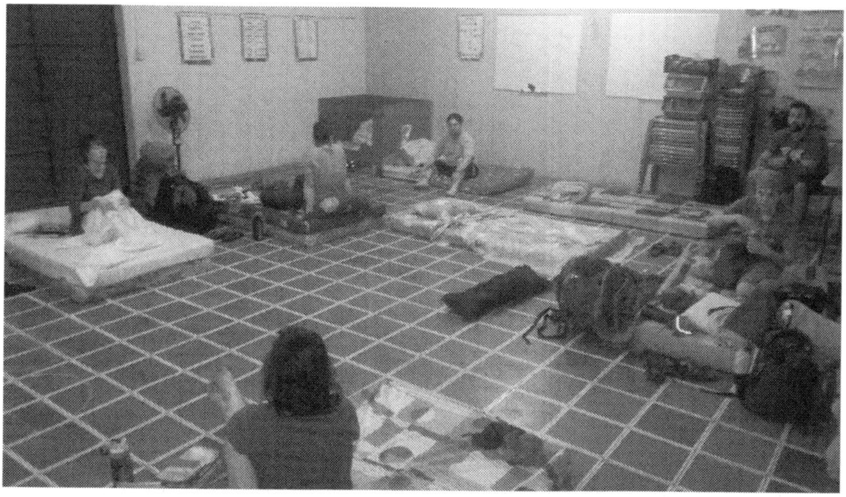

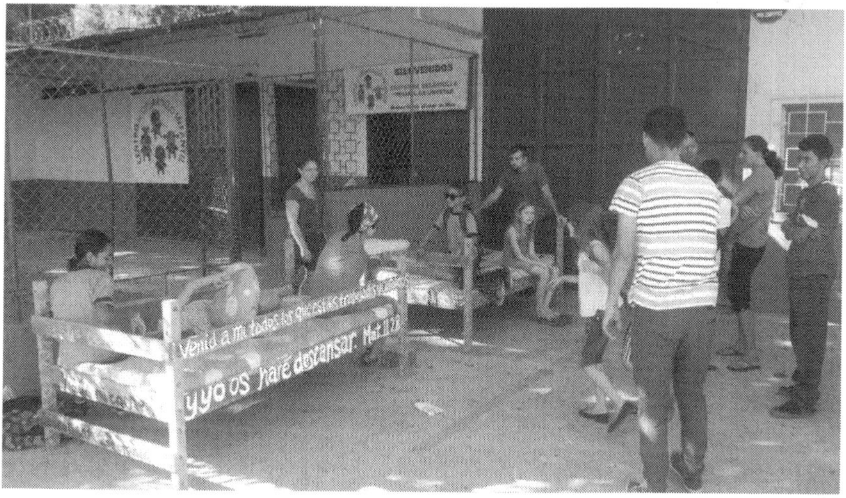
BIENVENIDOS
Venid a mi todos los
y yo os haré descansar.

Unexpected Greeting

A little girl said hi to Greg, Jeff, and I as we walked across the street bridge near our center. At first, we couldn't see who it was in the night's darkness. After spending a few minutes waving, but still trying to see through the obscurity, she became a little clearer. It was Anna, one of the children in our Child Development program we worked with all month. She stood still just long enough for us to recognize her, then scampered back off to play on the street.

Team Tear #3 – Jeff

Jeff Gala was the closest teammate I had in January. He was the only person whom I could look at and we'd both just start laughing because we knew what each other were thinking. Especially when "team time" or "feedback" or the girls were getting on our nerves in general.

With that being said, this tear story was one I did not anticipate or intend. On the last Wednesday of the month, Jeff shared with the team that he had decided to go home. He described being torn and struggling with being here daily ever since he'd arrived. We had joked together frequently about our frustrations with the trip because they were similar. It was not a surprise that he'd go home, but that it was so early.

He asked us for feedback after his explanation and the whole team graciously gave him positive affirmation for his decision, although we were all sad to see him go. Greg, our squad leader, asked me to close the night in prayer. I suggested we circle up and everyone pray over Jeff. I would close that.

Jeff was to my left, so he began the prayer by praying for our team. Each individual member of the team prayed for Jeff all the way around the circle. I closed by praying a prayer of thanks for the time I got to share with Jeff and being able to share my spirit with him. I prayed that it would go with him.

Jeff patted my shoulder with his hand that was draped across it. I closed the prayer by thanking God for directing our decisions as he does the waves and the wind. I thanked God for directing Jeff's decision to join the race and for his decision to go home. I thanked God for his Spirit that holds us together and for His love that unites us, which no distance or time can break.

As I said amen the circle broke, but Jeff and I still had our arms across each other's shoulders. With a few tears in his eyes, he said, "I love you, brother."

"I love you too, man. You'll always be a part of this team," I told him. We hugged one another. I stepped back to let the rest of the team hug him as well.

Team Tear #4 – Katrina

I woke up consistently earlier than the rest of the team in El Salvador. Throughout the month, my mornings seemed to come earlier each day. The day before we left I woke up well before dawn. I decided to walk down to the beach and try to see the sunrise. The beach was almost empty of any people. It was a perfectly calm morning. As the sun came up over the horizon, slowly reaching each building, bats would fly out and away from the sun's reach.

During the day, our team climbed a volcano. It was a beautiful journey to the top. Steam was seeping through the rocks at the top and if you stopped too long your shoes would melt. I decided that the next morning, for our team time we could watch the sunrise before leaving for Guatemala. After much complaining from our team, I said it was an optional team time. Only Alison and Katrina came with me the next morning.

They had the foresight to bring a couple bed sheets with them. We reached the beach early and they laid one bed sheet on the sand. They wrapped themselves up in the other one to keep warm. I sat down next to them. We waited quietly for a long time. We listened to the waves, watched the crabs, and saw the bats as the sun's rays reached over the horizon before the sun itself. As the sky became lighter, I decided to say some words I had thought to share.

I leaned on my arm in front of Alison and Katrina. I looked directly into Alison's eyes and put my hand on her foot. I told her that I was happy she's on my team. That I'm grateful for her cautious nature because I believe we will balance each other out nicely. I told her that I further am grateful for the way she cares so deeply for our team and that it is an inspiration for me to strive for.

She smiled throughout the time I was speaking to her. I smiled at her as I finished. I moved my hand to Katrina's foot. She smiled. I looked directly into her eyes and told her how grateful I was that she's on my team. I reinforced what I'd been saying to her all month: that she was a wonderfully kindred adventurous spirit. Her smile brightened. I then began to tell her that her love for her mom is incredible. I told her that the way she talks about her mom and expresses love for her is a phenomenal inspiration. That she has more love for her mom than I've seen in anyone else. Tears welled up in her eyes. I said to her that her love is an inspiration to me specifically and that I am going to try to love as she loves. With tears still in her eyes, she quietly said, "Thank you." We exchanged a smile.

I sighed and turned back around. The sun was already up. It must have been coming up as I was speaking to Alison and Katrina. I silently thanked God for timing the sun rising and my inclination to speak in sync. We sat silently a little while longer as the sun reached over the beach and pushed away the darkness behind us. Eventually, we stood and returned to the child development center that has been our home for the last month. We prepared to leave for Guatemala.

Favorite Moments in El Salvador

1. Eating 12 pupusas before Vladi cut me off
2. Hiking to the park, then to the waterfall
3. Petting the completely free bird behind the CDI with Brenna
4. Jumping into the waterfall pond, dropping off the branch into the water, drinking from the stream with Leah
5. Playing in the ocean together
6. Swimming out past the breakers and watching the sunset with Katrina
7. Wandering with Jeff and Greg into unknown neighborhoods at night
8. Allison and Katrina wrestling in masks
9. Acting out the skit on stage in the center of La Libertad
10. Hiking to the top and sliding into the active volcano

Photo courtesies: Brenna Lucero

PATRICK BOOTH

Guatemala

Summary

We began our second month with a week of debrief together. Our whole squad was getting to know one another as we relaxed following our first month in the field. This month largely felt like a blur to many of us. We had just begun to get comfortable with our teams and were now quickly thrust back into the window of meeting new people. Sure we had met at training camp and launch, but for many of us this was the time that we really began to build relationships outside of our team with the rest of the squad. It proved to be another double-edged sword. It was certainly nice to enjoy the time with a broader group of compatriots, but it also further delayed many from spending ample time with their teammates.

Personally, I enjoyed hearing from other squad mates about how their original teams were fairing with one another. I knew this time was limited and that soon enough we would be back solely with our teams again. I took every opportunity I could to spend time with people outside of my team. As the race has time specifically designed for team building, those relationships form as a matter of course. We had to choose to invest in anyone outside of our teams. This proved to be very important for me during this debrief and for every one of the debriefs that followed.

Life Lesson: Invest in individuals outside your immediate circles. Those relationships will be the ones that challenge you to grow the most.

My team found a nice balance of allowing space for individuals to invest in outside relationships while still making time to invest in one another. We met for team times typically about two or three times each week, giving us plenty of opportunity to press into one another. These team times could be anything from a Bible study to worshiping together to praying over one another. Each time we met, we would leave renewed with a stronger spirit. It was nice to have a team that chose to build each other up, even as we spent the majority of our time brandishing outside bonds.

This month provided us with some of the most available recreational excursions as well. Our host carpooled us into Antigua each weekend in order to enjoy the tourist atmosphere there. In Antigua we enjoyed pub crawls, salsa lessons, coffee bars, organic smoothies, as well as historic cathedrals, and their landmark memorial cross atop the hill. Five of us took an opportunity to enjoy Tikal, the Mayan capital city of the ancient world, one of these free weekends. Five others of us took the following weekend to enjoy Lago Atitlan, a lake surrounded by three volcanoes.

Service

This month was a balancing act between grounding our budding relationships with team members and trying to plant new relationships outside our teams. It was also a balancing act because in the first few days with GoMinistries our contact shared with us a five-year plan. A vision this broad tends to have an overwhelming effect on a group of 20-somethings planning to work with you for a mere month!

Our contact did an excellent job of letting us know that he didn't expect for everything he mentioned to get done while we were there, but he hoped that as much of it could get done as possible. With that, we were set to work!

The bulk of our work was with widows. We spent most of our days visiting widows' homes throughout Santo Domingo Xenacoj. A few times each week, we would venture further out to visit widows' homes in neighboring communities. These visits consisted of sharing gifts of rice or beans, spending some time chatting casually, asking to pray over them and their families, followed by occasional invitations to participate in whatever the next event our host had planned for the community.

We helped organize and facilitate multiple events for the widows. These events included worship songs together, a brief Bible message from our host, snacks and drinks, lots of hugging, playing with their children, giving out packages donated by Tom's Shoes, giving out eyeglasses donated through GoMinistries, and simply sharing fellowship with them throughout the communities.

School feeding programs made up the majority of our work apart from the widows we served. It is not customary for schools in Xenacoj to provide lunches for their students. Many of these students simply do not eat throughout the day while they are at school. Others simply do not eat for many days at a time.

For this reason, the family of the one staffer with GoMinistries would voluntarily make meals for hundreds of students. We would then visit schools with this staffer and serve food to hundreds of children who, otherwise, may very well not eat that day. At least a few members of our squad would help with this process 3-4 times a week. Occasionally, we would spend time after serving the food playing with the children or helping in their classrooms. Often this would be a project that ends around noonish, after which we would return to visiting widows for the remainder of the day.

Other service projects this month included:
- *exploring options to test viability for a barrel-ponics system*
- *compiling a book sharing our experience as a squad during the month*
- *spending time at schools playing with children*
- *teaching Bible lessons in schools*
- *teaching English in schools*
- *aiding teachers with their lessons in schools*
- *reaching out to community leaders, in order to connect GoMinistries with new communities.*

Claire's Healing

One night I woke up to hear a teammate vomiting in the bathroom just outside the men's dorm. I walked out partially to see what was going on and partially because I had to use the restroom. Claire was throwing up in the toilet and Katrina was sitting calmly next to her. (You could tell they're both nurses by their nonchalant demeanor given the circumstance.) Claire asked me from her knees if I had to use the bathroom. I told her no that would be awful to do. There was only one toilet. I got dressed, grabbed a key and walked a few blocks to our other dorm house to use the bathroom. I stopped for a minute on my way back in to tell Katrina not to hesitate if there's any way we can help, knowing there's nothing I could do.

I crawled back into bed feeling helpless. I prayed to God. Stating simply that he could do all things and my sister is suffering. I just want her to not suffer. I prayed that the illness would leave her body this night. That she would have restful sleep and awake revived. As I went to breakfast the next morning, I saw her sleeping soundly. When I came back she was up and about. She said she slept very well and awoke like she hadn't been sick at all.

Healing a Wounded Heart

There are often times that serving others in love does not look like the picture you imagined in your head. Today was one such experience for me. Throughout the month of February, we have served widows and children in Santo Domingo Xenacoj and the surrounding areas. This afternoon a small group of us visited Santa Maria. It was there that we visited a widow whose husband had passed away just yesterday.

When we arrived the widow was not present, but her family welcomed us into their home nonetheless to wait for her. As we sat down, we noticed a few plastic cups and an empty bottle of some kind of liquor. A man came up to introduce himself and thank us for the visit. It seemed difficult to communicate with him, even beyond the usual difficulty many of us had with Spanish. Two other family members, a woman and a man, explained that he was deaf and he was the father of the man who died. I was amazed at how he could smile after such a tragic loss, but he did not stop saying how grateful he was for us sharing love with his family during their time of grief.

The second man began to draw my attention at this time. He explained through many slurred words that his heart was hurting this day. He expressed sadness that weighed like a heavy burden upon him. Stumbling to a stool beside me, he told me that he and his brothers had been trying to salve their wounded hearts with alcohol for the better part of the day. Their hearts were heavy because there had been four brothers and now there were only three. The one who passed away had always been the one to bring them together and now they were unsure of their family's strength. Nevertheless, he said that it was a great inspiration to them that we would visit them during this difficult time.

At this point, my Spanish had long since failed me. It was time that I ask for help by someone with a little more understanding. I turned to one of the girls who spoke Spanish fluently. As I did this,

I noticed the unease on the rest of the team's faces and realized I was the only man in the group. My teammate, Betsy, pushed through her unease. She came to sit down next to the drunk, grieving brother and me. As he began to realize that she was translating to me, he began to talk more directly to her. Betsy leaned back in her chair to both avoid the spittle coming out of his mouth and the way that he leaned in much too close for comfort.

Occasionally, when it seemed necessary, I would place a hand on his shoulder and say, *"Lo siento para ti y tu familia* (I'm sorry for you and your family)." This would briefly redirect his attention to me and he would routinely express gratitude for our sympathy. During one of these instances, I told him that his brother would live on in his heart. It was the first time I saw peace in his eyes. He responded by saying we are all brothers.

Briefly after this, he asked where all of us were from and which church we came with. Betsy and I stated which state each teammate was from. I told him we were with the Iglesia de German. (German is our ministry contact who organizes the care for children and widows in Guatemala through GoMinistries.) The widow arrived at this time. German expressed sorrow to her for her loss and provided gifts of food to her. We sang her a song, then prayed for her and her family. As we began to leave, the grieving brother shook each of our hands and said, *"Muchas gracias."*

As he shook my hand I stated once again that his brother would live on in his heart and placed my hand on his chest. He put his hand on my shoulder and said, *"Muchas gracias, mi hermano* (Thank you, my brother)."

"Siempre (Always)," I said with my hand still over his heart.

"Siempre." He smiled through his tears.

Three different girls on my team came up to me afterwards and thanked me for being there. They said that my presence distracted him from them and they were grateful for this because they were very uneasy with the situation. I was very grateful for the opportunity to serve my team in this way and, as always, I was grateful to do what little we could to ease the pain of a suffering widow. But more than anything, I was grateful this day to be able to be a brother, for a brief window of time, to a man who had just lost his own.

Unexpected Greeting

While Katrina and I were walking in Santo Domingo Xenacoj a little boy exclaimed, "Patricio!" He and his sister then came running up to hug Katrina and me. As they ran off, I asked her if she recognized them.

"No. They certainly knew you though," she replied.
We were about a block away from the school we had fed a few days earlier.

Forget the World Race

Throughout this month in Guatemala I have been grateful to witness many wonderful blessings:

***

A few teammates and I went to visit a widow in her home. As Jarrad, Kathryn, Dani, and I entered the widow's home, Dani immediately received a fervent hug from the widow's granddaughter. The little girl remained close to Dani throughout the visit, often repeating the hugging process and joyously bouncing about. This boundless joy spread to the little girl's parents and to her grandmother, evident by the shared smiles throughout the room. It was explained that the little girl had met missionaries before and Dani resembled one that became very close to the little girl.

As I watched them interact with one another, I knew that the little girl did not only recognize the appearance of the previous missionary. She also recognized a kind heart filled with love; she recognized a Spirit shared by these two people who had come all the way across the world simply to show love to her family. As we left, the little girl and her friend came with us. We began to walk to a park to play with them, and then Dani wished aloud that she could buy them some ice cream or something. Jarrad pulled his wallet out and joyfully shared what he had. I had a meeting to go to so Jarrad and I said our goodbyes, leaving Dani and Kathryn each sitting with a little girl beside them on one of the many benches. From the time we had originally arrived to my last look behind me, I never saw the little girls stop smiling.

***

A wonderful man named German and his family hosted us throughout the month. German guided our work with the local widows and orphans. He took us directly to each house, provided gifts of corn or beans to give to them, told us their needs and organized our visits to feed many schools. His family took care of any needs we had for housing, cooked our food, and cared for us as though we were no further from kin to them. I regularly observed Kelly, my teammate, going to their house before the food was presented. I complimented her on this and she humbly said that often she ends up just chatting with them, rather than helping make the food. As the month went on, I noticed she was going over to their house at times when no food was being prepared. She became more than a helper to them and had grown far from someone they were there to serve. Kelly built a relationship with German's family based on shared experience, compassion, and love. It is with these building blocks that a kingdom that cares for one another throughout the world can be built.

***

While singing, worshipping, and sharing community with German's family one night, he asked for one or two volunteers to help him if they desired. My hand immediately went up. Jarrad stated as we were walking back to our house that he would like to go as well. The next morning we met German at his house at 5:30 a.m. to go check on a donation that had been offered to him from a priest in another city. He expressed that this was a significant blessing because he had never received offerings of donations from local priests before. As we began our journey from Santo Domingo Xenacoj to Guatemala City, he stopped to pick up his brother. This was a pleasant surprise, which afforded Jarrad and I lots of opportunity to practice our Spanish because German's brother spoke no English whatsoever!

We drove up to a seminary school and were invited inside. As we were led around the corner, we spotted dozens of boxes stacked on top of one another. After a few moments, I pointed out to Jarrad that the boxes were labeled "Tom's". Sure enough, as the boxes were opened, these were shoes donated by Tom's Shoes to the seminary school. They were given more than they needed, so they shared about 150 pairs of shoes with us to give freely to the widows we served in Xenacoj.

"It's pretty cool to be on the other side of this process," Jarrad commented. I had to agree.

As we made our two-hour journey back, German joked that Jarrad was buying us all breakfast. Then German asked us where we would like to stop. As he went to pay, Jarrad again pulled his own money out of his pocket. It was a wonderful way to say thank you for all of the kindness that German and his family had shared with us. But more than that, it was a wonderful breakfast in which we got to speak more candidly and comfortably with German and his brother. They shared concerns that mirrored our concerns; we shared joys that mirrored their joys. It was a lesson in the universal nature that is shared by all of us. As I shook German's brother's hand goodbye and he cupped his other hand around mine, I knew I was saying goodbye to a kindred spirit.

***

In Santa Cruz Ayapan, our whole squad was spending time playing with a school full of children. I noticed one of my teammates, Amanda, in a group of children by herself. As I went to join her, she was asking them how many of them knew the guitar. A few hands went up excitedly. She next asked who wants to play the guitar. More hands went up with more excitement.
She jogged off towards the van we came in on. The kids began to ask me if I could do backflips. As I said no, they seemed disappointed. (I found out later Amanda had been entertaining them with gymnastics.) She came running back with her guitar. The kids swarmed her!

She asked, "Who wants to play it?" Every hand went up! As she pushed hands away from her face, I motioned for the children to move back and commanded, "*Más espacio! Más espacio para ella!* (More space! More space for her!)" The children moved back a little, but every hand was still pressed forward as close as possible.

Amanda told the children to close their eyes. She chose a hand at random and allowed them to play her guitar with her hands guiding theirs. She repeated this process one more time. This time, after she chose the hand at random, she said, "*Abre tus ojos* (Open your eyes)." The child said he couldn't. She instructed again for the child to open his eyes. The other children said he couldn't because he was blind. She reached out and took his hand. She guided his hands to her guitar and with her help he played beautifully. That child shone more brightly than any star I have ever seen. As we were called back to the van to prepare to leave, Amanda and I thanked the Holy Spirit for his guidance to the hand that needed the music the most.

***

One night, we hosted an invitational widow gathering for singing, food, and fellowship at our house. We were amazed as widows never stopped coming throughout the night. Although the gathering was meant to have started at 6:30 p.m., we were searching for more seats to borrow from neighboring houses after filling all we had at 8:30 p.m.

One of the last widows to arrive was especially moving to see come join us; she was riding in her wheelchair, being pushed up to our house by her daughter as night drew darker. As the service closed and the widows left, I made my acquaintance with her and her family. As we talked, I helped wheel her out into the street. Her daughter expressed gratitude for the help and I asked her if she would like me to push her all the way home. "*Sí!*" she exclaimed gratefully.

So we began to walk down the hill together. I hollered at my squad leader, Greg, to come walk with me and he obliged with graciousness. As we walked, the family and I talked about my journey for starting the race, how the mission was going, what it was like to travel to so many places and serve in love. They expressed significant gratitude for the care we showed the widows in the community, expressing how difficult it can be for them without help. Eventually, they asked how we would travel from one country to another. I joked that Greg was the boss and only he knew. They smiled. Greg joked that he was taking a bus, but I would be walking. They laughed uproariously!

I cannot express what a joy it is to see people who have suffered greatly experience happiness because of something as simple as the words you share with them. After reaching the widow's house, we said our goodbyes. As we walked across the city back to our house, I told Greg that was one of the best experiences I'd had in Guatemala. Wisely, he encouraged me to share that with the squad; it would be good for everyone to hear how wonderful it is to go the extra mile.

***

These experiences and many others have demonstrated to me that this journey is not about what Adventures in Missions tells us it will be about. It will not be about what the contacts we are visiting have prepared for us to do. I have not been called to accept opportunities that are presented to me. I have been called to create opportunities to love and serve others. My service will never be in the boat that the World Race committee has built for me. My service will be out there in the waves where people don't have a voice to cry for help because they are drowning. I will have the faith to walk out onto the water. I will put my hands down beneath the depths. I will pull them up.

Betsy's Coat

During a final weekend excursion in Guatemala, five of us had headed out to Lago Atitlan. It was Kathryn, Kelly, Brenna and Betsy, and I. We booked two nights in a hostel right on the water.

The first day had been a nice relaxing experience of getting to know our surroundings. We had walked up the hill to the town, got dinner from a street vendor and sat down from our higher vantage point to take in the lake's view while we were eating. We came back to our hostel that night and played pool while talking about our travel dreams until the night put us all to bed.

The next morning we opted to take a short hike up a trail that rounds the lake along the mountainside reaching a neighboring town. It proved to be far longer than we expected!

We ventured up and down the mountainside. Our steps took us across planks that had been made so the trail could cross the water. A guide coming out of a village we passed through admonished us not to stop there.

"This is a dangerous town for outsiders."

Finally, four hours after we embarked on our "twenty-minute" trail, we reached the town on the other side. We stopped to have pizza since we were all starving. It would give us time to rest indeed; the woman who greeted us took our order, then went to go start the fire. After she got the fire going strong, she began to prepare the food. We enjoyed our respite.

It was a short walk to a taxi dock that could return us to our original hostel. We were all very glad of this!

That night we all just wanted to relax a little. Kelly, Kathryn and I went into a sweat lodge the hostel had on site. (It's like a wet sauna, but hotter.)

The calm would only last so long.

After some time, we began to hear Brenna and Betsy speaking surprisingly urgently. Then we heard crying.

We came out to find that Betsy's grandmother's body had

begun to shut down from the inside out. Betsy was balling. It was clear that she had lots of love for her grandmother.

But grieving over such a distance can be a difficult thing. One asks themself:

"Should I have been there?"

"Should I go home?"

"What could I do if I were there?"

"Would it make a difference?"

To make matters more complicated, we were five hours away from the rest of the squad. The rest of the squad was two hours away from the nearest airport.

We tried our best to be there for Betsy that night. We prayed for her, for her family and for her grandmother. We hugged her. We let her know we would support her in any way she asked.

Betsy had spoken with her family over the phone. She had expressed her love. She decided that she would return with us the next day, as had originally been planned.

The next morning we all prepared to leave first thing in the morning. We waited by the dock for our water taxi to arrive. Betsy told us that she had been debating in the night if she should go home or not. She resolved to leave it to God.

Betsy had left her coat on our first water taxi ride out to our hostel two days prior. She had all but given up on finding it again. She said that she had asked God to give her a sign to go home or stay. If she were able to recover her coat it would mean to hold home, if she was not it would mean she should stay.

As she told us this, our original water taxi from two days prior pulled up to the dock. We climbed on and asked him about coat. He said that another couple on the boat had taken her coat. He ferried us to their hostel, where they were sitting right out on the patio. Betsy walked up and asked them as we waited in the boat. She returned saying they had dropped it off at our hostel. The boat driver graciously ferried us back to our hostel and Betsy hopped off into their office. We waited as Betsy went inside to check on it.

She came out with a glowing smile. "I'm going home," she told us. She pulled her coat over her shoulders.

***

This seemed remarkable enough, but we would later see that God clearly had a plan for her trip home all along.

Betsy had a connecting flight from Atlanta to Nashville on her way home and noticed the passenger next to her speaking in Spanish. It turned out they were not only on the flight to the States together. He was returning to Honduras (this was our next country) on the same flight she was planning to take after her brief time at home.

He explained that he was a pastor of a church in Honduras. She explained that she was serving for eleven months on the mission field. As they talked more about this, she shared that her team would be doing Unsung Heroes with their time in Honduras. This means that they were seeking new contacts for Adventures in Missions to work with.

His church had ample opportunity for volunteer service and was able to host teams in exchange. This became the first contact their team would work with in Honduras. The rest of the team met the pastor a few days after Betsy returned to the field.

The pastor's church has gone on to become a working partner with Adventures in Missions.

THE LONG ROAD HOME

Favorite Moments in Guatemala

1. Barhopping in Antigua
2. Visiting Tikal
3. Hiking around Lago Atitlan
4. Experiencing the best worship session I've ever been a part of during all-night prayer vigil with Karissa and Mel Jo
5. Sharing stories with the squad during lunch

PATRICK BOOTH

Honduras

Summary

This month began a little unusually. Our entire squad traveled together to the capital city and there we met our host for the month. We were informed we would have a long drive ahead of us. Our host stopped at a local mall and offered us lunch while he and his wife met their daughter there for a quick visit. We then piled into the vehicle and began our journey to Catacamas, Olancho. The drive proved to be just as long as they said it would be! We stopped once along the way before arriving well into the morning hours on a Saturday night.

The next morning we would be attending church with our host. We asked if there is anything we need to have prepared. They responded without hesitation that we would need to be ready to sing two songs: one in Spanish and one in English. Their demeanor told us they were not joking. So we took a few minutes to select some familiar songs; graciously they gave us till the following week to perform them anyway.

We also asked if there is anything we need to know about the typical dress. They took a brief look at the grisly bearded men on our team and then joked that we would need to cut our hair, shave our faces, put on some ties, etc. (Don't worry. This time they smiled slightly while they were giving their response, which seemed to indicate to us that they were not too serious.)

Nevertheless, the next morning when they returned, I had shaved my face completely. The surprised look on our host pastor's face betrayed his shock, despite his cool composure. His wife, on the other hand, made no note of any change... It wasn't until we were all eating lunch after the church service together that she recognized who I was! She exclaimed she thought her memory had simply been mistaken and she was meeting a different person than she remembered from the night before!

Honduras was far and away one of the most comfortable months we had in the field. Our top priority in ministry was aiding teachers in a bilingual school that was owned and operated by the church we were working with. We again had a nice work schedule that allowed for plenty of time to relax between service hours. We were informed during the first week that we would be working with the school Monday through Friday, would work Saturday mornings with a feeding program for poor mothers and children, and would sing songs routinely each Sunday morning at church services.

Service

Our squad leader, Ashley Francis, mentioned to us that the World Race has a policy of requesting at least one full day off at each mission location. Our team briefly glanced around at each other and then responded that we will be happy to serve in every way we are asked to. When you love your work, it never feels like an obligation. Our workdays during the week established a comfortable routine:

7:00 - 8:00 a.m.
*We would make ourselves breakfast and usually have a short devotional or prayer of some kin*d.

8:00 -11:30 a.m.
We took turns in different classrooms, working with different teachers. In this school, teachers rotated classrooms and the students in each grade level stay in the same room throughout the day. Some days we would stay in the room and work different subjects with the same students, while other days we would rotate with the teachers as they taught the different grade levels the same subject, such as mathematics, science, reading, or social studies.

11:30 a.m. -1:00 p.m.
The school provided lunch for many of the students, as well as for us. We would eat with them and the teachers together. Any free time allowed after that would be for playing with the children out on the playground or soccer field.

1:00 - 3:00 p.m.
Classes would resume and we continued to aid the teachers throughout the day.

The rest of the day was left to our discretion. We would usually relax for a brief time in the afternoon before coming together again for dinner, which we prepared for ourselves. Most days, following dinner we would share a brief team time. These consisted of anything from watching movies to deep dialogues and swimming in the pool or sharing stories from our classrooms with our teammates.

***

Each Saturday we walked down to a feeding program that took place to aid mothers and children with low or, in most cases, no income. This would start around nine-thirty in the morning with a brief worship service, followed by games with the children, and then the meal would be between eleven and noon. After that, we would help pack and clean everything back up. Sometimes we would walk with the mothers and children back some of the way along the street towards their homes, but we would almost always be finished for the day around one or two in the afternoon.

Every Sunday we would be picked up by a member of the congregation or church staff and brought to the church service. We would perform an English and Spanish song most Sundays to the delight of the congregation present. Usually we would join the pastor for lunch after this and then would be returned to the church's retreat center, which was made our home for the month.

Extra opportunities this month included:

- *building relationships with Nacho, our groundskeeper, and his family*
- *performing songs and conducting interviews for the church's radio/TV show*
- *spending time with long-term missionaries residing in Catacamas*
- *helping put together a Father's Day event for the students' parents*
- *hosting a "pool day" with the children from the feeding programs*
- *aiding in a field trip with the school to historic cavesites*

Team Tear #5 – Leah

Today I shared with my team a reason I'd been fasting from everything except lunch for the first week here in Honduras. We had had a discussion about groceries and the lunches at our school cost us $2.50 each. We were allotted $4/day for food. A spirit of fear permeated the discussion even though we resolved that the budget was manageable. I wanted to demonstrate that we would be fine with whatever food we are provided.

But I extended my fast and changed its purpose this morning. I shared with the team that my unborn niece's heart is developing slowly and they are expecting to have to do surgery in the first few months. I will not eat any food except the lunches provided at the school until my niece's due date on March 27 [three weeks away].

The team asked to pray for my niece and family immediately. One by one, they opened their prayers to my brother, my sister-in-law, and my unborn niece. I couldn't help but be moved by their prayers. Leah wept as she prayed for a miracle. This is the only time she had cried during any prayer. She prayed that the team had talked about how wonderful it would be to witness a miracle and she prayed that this would be the one to occur, even if it is happening 2000 miles away. After the prayer, every team member gave me a hug. As I hugged Leah, I told her, "Your prayers are supernatural."

"I think the emotion was too," she said. "I don't know where that came from." She said it was really cool that I was actually petitioning God for something, rather than just fasting for the sake of fasting.

Leah and I had a feedback session two nights prior where we were instructed to partner up, speak life into one another, and pray for each other. We were the last ones to go bed that night.

Juan Carlos

As we exited the church service, our pastor's truck pulled up to greet us outside the doors. A man unknown to us stepped out of the driver's door and opened the other doors for us. "Adelante (Come in)," he encouraged. It was not uncommon for the pastor to have someone else drive us home using his vehicle, so we climbed in thinking nothing extraordinary. As we began our drive home, my teammate encouraged me to ask the man his name.

"*Cuál es su nombre, amigo?* (What is your name, friend?)" I asked.

He responded, "Juan Carlos."

He went on to say that he had a question for us. He prefaced his question with the assertion that he had heard one of us was a counselor. Sitting in the center behind him, I confirmed that I was the counselor he had heard about. He then went on to explain that he has a son attending the school that is our main ministry for this month. His name is Juan Carlos also.

"Juan Carlos Gomez," I affirm.

I immediately know whom he is talking about. His son is on a list of children with discipline problems I have been provided by the principal. He further explains that his son does not care to do his homework or study while in class. This father describes a torn heart because he does not want to punish his child constantly, but also wants him to do better in school. He illustrates that it is not a lack of capability because the boy works hard on his grandfather's farm and knows more about the farm than many of the men who help do the work. Young Juan Carlos loves his grandpa's farm. So much so, that a story is told about taking away the time at his grandpa's farm recently because of poor grades. Our driver expresses discomfort saying that he knows this hurt his son because his son cried that day. But he says that he knows that with the grace of God and with my help, his son can do better.

***

Now there is a pause felt in the air. This man is waiting for a divine revelation that can turn his world around. He sits waiting to hear it from a man that has never had children. I silently long for the wisdom to give this man peace. Then I begin speaking. I explain to Juan Carlos that I had just worked with his son today in physical education for a few hours. He participated well in that class (admittedly, I left out that most kids participate well in physical education). I complimented Juan Carlos on taking away the privilege of visiting his grandfather's farm, especially since this seems to be something he cares about greatly. I encouraged Juan Carlos to remember that his child's punishments should evoke discomfort, because if they do not he will not change his behavior. Although it is difficult to see that combination of anger and sadness in his child, it is exactly these emotions that will remind him to do better next time.

I continue to give the best advice I can muster about providing positive rewards, such as going to grandpa's farm only when young Juan Carlos has had a full week without problems in school. My focus moves toward the Juan Carlos in front of me, driving my team and I home. I explain to him that children are going through many emotional changes as they grow up and that a natural part of this process is for them to rebel against authority. Juan Carlos nods his head. I illustrate that despite the changes his son will go through, a consistent discipline and reward system at home will take deeper root than the changing world around him. Juan Carlos' eyes glance at me in the mirror. I reinforce that this lesson will be important for his son in life, as well as at school because, if executed well, it will teach him that hard work and diligence provides greater rewards than immediate personal satisfaction. Juan Carlos shakes his head once in agreement then repeatedly as he exhales deeply.

I close the conversation by saying I am happy to see Juan Carlos taking such an interest in his son's education because, despite his rebellion, his son will model his father's behavior. I tell Juan Carlos that he is doing a great job and encourage him as a parent to have patience. Although some lessons will be learned slower than others, his patience will be a blessing to his child.

We are now pulling up to our gate and another teammate has jumped out of the truck to open it up. Juan Carlos turns around to me and says simply, "Gracias." A few minutes later, he is saying his goodbyes to the whole team, as is custom here in Latin America.

***

I wish I could tell you that the next day when I saw Juan Carlos Gomez he was the best behaved kid in class. I wish I could tell you that I am certain my words inspired understanding and peace in his father. I wish I could tell you that the course of a little boy's life was changed because the course of his relationship with his father took a blessed turn.

But I can't.

Sometimes we cannot see the horizon and although we don't feel it, the world is constantly turning. I may not have tilted the axis of this man's life as he had hoped for, but I pray that my words were able to give him the encouragement he needed to continue on for one more rotation.

Ashley's Throat

In Honduras, Ashley had told us a few times about how she has problems with her esophagus closing up on her in response to certain foods. It didn't seem to be a problem most of the time. One day however, as we were eating together on the last day with the teachers, she subtly asked Ryan and I to pray for her. She said she was having troubles, but did not want it to be a big deal. We took a moment to silently pray individually. She visibly paused a moment, then said, "Thanks, guys." She told us later that she had instantly felt better. Even more so, that her throat did not give her any more problems for the rest of that day.

Unexpected Greeting

As the team was walking back from visiting a cross overlook, a little boy called my name out from behind our group. We all stopped and turned to see who was trying to get our attention. He then came running up to hug me. He was one of the children I had taught in the bilingual school.

Favorite Moments in Honduras

1. Getting Ash Fran to use Jeff's towel that Ryan had used all race without washing on a 1-200 dare (sweet 157)

    Ashley introduced us to a game called "What are the odds?" It's a simple dare game where the person being dared picks the odds of having to do the task. After the odds are chosen, an objective person counts down to three, and then the darer and daree both say a number. If the number is the same, the dare must be followed through with.

    Jeff had left during El Salvador. Ryan had used his towel ever since without ever washing it. Ash was the next person to use it after my dare!

2. Paying the price for it when she caught me on the 1-15, peeing in the sleeping bag on their doorstep

    Ashley had vengeance on her mind for days. She remembered the worst dare she had ever witnessed on another squad. Someone was dared to urinate in their own sleeping bag. She dared me and I lost.

    I would honor my agreement. And just to make sure that the girls knew I lived up to my word, I left the sleeping bag on their doorstep.

3. Climbing the mango tree, chatting with the two kids that joined us, then watching the sun set beyond the mountains behind the mango tree
4. Sharing the mango tree with the team
5. Swimming with the teachers and pastor's family
6. Being invited to and giving a lesson on codependency during our first Leadership Development Conference

    We met as an entire squad for three days to share important lessons before moving on to Nicaragua.

Nicaragua

Summary

Nicaragua provided the most Spirit-filled month I would have on the Race. It has a bit of a back-story:

About a week or two before we were finished with our time in Honduras, we were informed that we would not have a squad leader with us during our next month. We were given our contact information for Nicaragua and I was asked to be the point man to make contact with our host. So, during that next week, I gave him a call and he told me he had no idea we were coming. He went on to tell me that emails had been exchanged, but no details had been confirmed for date, times, number of people, etc.

Needless to say, this came as a bit of a surprise. I asked about the possibility of our team coming to work with him, to which he replied that he would not be there in Nicaragua during the time allotted so it simply could not be worked out. He was very gracious and said he could connect us with other missionary friends he has in the country that would likely be able to work with us. However, the administration at Adventures in Missions would opt to go in a different direction. To this day, I am very grateful that they chose to follow a different path.

After some talks between Ashley and the home base in Georgia, we were instructed not to worry about it. We simply raised our hands and trusted they were pulling something else together. They were.

We had a short Leadership Development Workshop between Honduras and Nicaragua. This was a few days that the squad and leaders met together to discuss ways to enhance the race experience for all of us. During a lunch with the leadership there, we were asked if we would like to take this opportunity to do something they had not done in years. It was something they called an "Ask The Lord" month. It was described as an opportunity to pray to God each day, to listen intently to His Spirit, and to carry out the callings in whatever way we believe necessary. Our team was all very excited immediately. Nevertheless, we took some time that afternoon to pray about it and to discuss it amongst ourselves. After this, our excitement had grown, rather than diminished. We thanked the leaders for their trust and faith in us. We thanked them for the opportunity.

    We said yes.

Granada

1) On day two, we decided we'd take care of our errands before starting a prayer walk through the city the following day. Despite this, the Spirit had other plans. As Brenna and I were setting up our SIM cards for the team phones, Leah and Katrina walked through a nearby park. After finishing with the cell phones, we found the two of them sitting down praying with an elderly woman. It was clear the language barrier had hardly limited their interaction. Neither Leah nor Katrina speaks Spanish well enough to carry a full conversation, but the woman's smile and joyful embrace of each of them afterwards seemed to say words simply aren't as important as we imagine.

2) Near Granada there is a men's home for people overcoming alcohol and drug addiction. It is more of a discipling program because it is nine months, more time than usually used simply to maintain sobriety. Ryan and I visited this home on Good Friday. The program had just started a couple weeks before. There were three men there attending. Mario was one of these three men; he speaks English and is a translator by trade.

I poured out hope to these men. I assured them that they would be a great hope and inspiration to many men that will be coming to the program later. We enjoyed a worship service together along with visitors from the local village, and then watched the *Passion of the Christ*. After this we had dinner together, then I asked to pray for these men. I prayed for their faithfulness to be the men God wants them to be, I thanked God for the wonderful works He would do in and through their lives, I prayed for the program and asked for blessings upon it, as well as thanking God for the incredible servant's heart of the program director. (The program director set the program up after recovering from addiction himself.)

These men's families would be visiting the coming Sunday. Mario said he was afraid he might be too hard on his daughter who is getting into trouble. I prayed grace over him and assured him that his concern would certainly stifle him from being too rigid.

***

Our team practiced listening prayer throughout our time in Granada. We felt called to leave after three days, in order to head towards San Juan Del Sur. All of the hostels we called were overbooked due to Semana Santa. (Semana Santa means Holy Week. It is the week before Easter and is heavily celebrated throughout many countries in Latin America. It is akin to Carnaval in Rio de Janeiro or Mardi Gras in New Orleans.) We booked our transportation for the day before Easter...

...without a destination in San Juan Del Sur.

Learning Forgiveness

Ask The Lord was our ministry this month. After having a ministry contact fall through on the first month, our team was left without a team leader and we were asked by Adventures in Mission if we would be comfortable doing a month of seeking His Spirit. Our team was very excited to answer the call.

We started our month in Granada, Nicaragua. After a day or two of prayer, a couple teammates shared that they had received the number three. We decided to leave the city after three days. As we began to pray for our next calling, signs began to point us towards San Juan Del Sur. We were advised by a local contact in Granada to wait a few days for Semana Santa to be over, as it would be dangerous to be in San Juan Del Sur during the holiday season.

We had already booked our transportation by that time and wanted to answer the calling we'd received. We arrived in San Juan Del Sur on the Saturday before Easter. As we searched for a hostel, we found one that was cheaper than all the others we'd seen. The price was changed after we moved our stuff in. It was still cheaper than any other, but the underhanded change enraged my teammate, Ryan, and myself. We resolved to stay there anyway and find a new hostel in the next few days.

Later that evening, the hostel owner told us the price would drop in half the next night because Semana Santa would be over. I witnessed an immediate change in the way our team interacted with her from then on, myself included. We challenged ourselves to practice forgiveness more readily in the future. This was an opportunity that we would not have had if we had come a day later. I believe it was the reason for our calling on that day.

The team responded well to the lesson in forgiveness. Ryan asked if he could buy us all coffee that next morning and surprisingly invited the hostel owner as well. She joined us for coffee and when she heard we were going to Easter service afterwards, she decided to come with us. After the service, she introduced us to her daughter living across the street, whose birthday was on Easter. We prayed for her and her daughter then returned to the hostel.

***

A few days ago, while practicing silent listening prayer, it seemed significant that this lesson in forgiveness was revealed to us on Easter. **Forgiveness brings new life.** As I contemplated this, I thought of my new niece, Hannah Grace, who is struggling early in her new life. I prayed for opportunities to practice forgiveness, so that new life may be brought forth and gifted to her. I received my answer to this prayer last night.

While our team sat enjoying a dessert on a dining patio Alison exclaimed, "Leah! Your purse!" We all looked to see her purse on the sand on the other side of the balcony with a little boy standing over it. I perched on the balcony while Katrina walked down the steps to pick it up. The little boy made no motions toward the purse, but rather turned and ran away. Unfortunately, checking the purse, we discovered Alison's cash and debit card had already been taken out.

There was a mixed air in our team after that. A mixture of anger for the incident and pity that this would be done by a little boy. I felt a conviction to pray and we did. I prayed that Leah would not feel responsible, that Alison would be secure that God and her team family will provide for her needs, and for the little boy I prayed that God would work in his heart and life so that he may live in a new way.

This morning, as the sun was rising, I prayed in a way I haven't prayed before. I prayed that God would fulfill His prophecy revealed to me in a dream many years ago, where I picked up a dead bird and it flew away. I prayed that healing power would be imparted today and Hannah would be the first recipient. I spoke to God with confidence, reminding Him that His lesson taught me forgiveness brings new life. That I had asked for opportunities to forgive and that He had answered. I exclaimed to Him that He had spoken into my heart to pray for the boy last night and I had responded in kind. He placed it upon my heart to share the story this morning and so this blog is being sent out now.

I call upon God for healing as He has promised. I pray for a miracle because I know that You can do it. I ask the Lord not to bring peace during this time of hardship, but rather to bring a supernatural healing to end this time of hardship. In a new way I ask the Lord.

Jennyfer

After Leah and Ryan had received the number three during listening prayer, our team decided to leave Granada after three days. We went to San Juan Del Sur despite receiving admonitions that we should wait until after Semana Santa (which is a lot like spring break in the U.S.). We promptly met Jennyfer, who was the owner of the hostel we were staying at.

Our relationship with Jennyfer grew throughout the month. Ryan graciously invited her for coffee with us on Easter. Leah then asked if she attends church and she responded by volunteering to come with us to Easter service. After this, she introduced us to her daughter. Since it was her daughter's birthday we offered a prayer for the two of them together.

One week later it was Jennyfer's birthday. We took her some sweet bread. She invited us back for cake later that evening. She welcomed us and shared dessert with us, saying she was happy we could be with her on this special day. Ryan was back home in Texas at this time. She mentioned she is diabetic and needed something for that, asking if he could bring some back. We said we would ask if it was possible. We prayed for her before leaving.

Another week later, we stopped in while taking a worship walk. Ryan had brought Moringa Powder for himself and the team. He thought he could give some to her, since it is a health booster. There were some hesitations in the team because we didn't know its effects in regards to people with diabetes. We looked it up online and learned Moringa Powder is a recommended homeopathic remedy for diabetes.

She was happy to receive the gift. We sang a few songs for her and prayed again for her before moving on.

Lydiette

Leah and Allison had a significant impact on one of the ladies, Lydiette, working at our second hostel in San Juan del Sur. As they discussed with her their work as missionaries, she spoke with an air of guilt that she was not Christian. Despite this, throughout their conversation she expressed many beliefs of Christianity as her own.

They discovered she simply meant she does not attend church. They assured her that she could be Christian without attending church. They spoke life and hope into her, freeing her from a rigid legalistic view of Christianity.

After this conversation, I saw Leah helping with some of the lady's work from time to time. At these times, I saw a new air of confidence and joy in the woman's demeanor.

One day Allison and Leah took Lydiette out for coffee. She told them that it meant the world to her because she works all the time and has little time for friends. It probably meant that much more that people who are staying in the hostel where she works wanted to take their own time to spend with her.

The next day she brought them mangoes she had picked fresh from a tree in her yard, simply as an act of kindness.

Their experiences with Lydiette are a beautiful reminder that no matter the nature of our relationships, we always have the opportunity to incorporate more love into each and every one of them. Thanks for the lesson, ladies.

Tom

 I took a "man night" for myself on the Saturday Ryan was out of town. I went to a local fight night and met a guy there from Sweden who was traveling alone. We talked about punk music, boxing, seeing friends waste away in addiction, and countless other shared experiences. Although Tom is an atheist, I immediately felt he was a kindred spirit. I bought him a beer, for which he seemed very grateful. He seemed grateful not for the beer, but simply the gesture of kindness.

 He invited me to come surfing with him the next day and said he was gonna try hitchhiking to the beach. I was apprehensive and replied with a maybe. The next day, I felt I should follow up. I walked into his hostel after church and he greeted me immediately. The girls prayed safety over me, and then Tom and I set out to find us a ride. The second car driving by picked us up. It went all the way to the beach. I spent that day surfing and discovering more of our shared ideals.

 As the day was closing, Tom joked that his friends at home would never believe he had such a great time with a missionary. I suggested he open the story every time with, "So I met this missionary at fight night..." With a laugh, he said he surely would. As we approached his hostel, he mentioned a raw vegan restaurant that he wanted to try.

 Two days later, our team was walking around setting up dinner plans. They wanted to try the raw vegan place too, but it was closed. We happened to run into Tom walking in the street. We made plans to meet him the next night for dinner at the restaurant.

 The next day our team hiked up a hill to a Jesus statue overlooking San Juan Del Sur. Tom joined us for dinner that evening. As we prayed over the food, he mentioned it was the first time he'd experienced that. During dinner together, Tom mentioned that he wanted to make the hike to the statue he'd seen up on the hill. I offered to lead the way for him the next day and invited any of the team to join us. He was grateful to have a guide and some company to make the hike. Our team picked up the tab for dinner and Tom again expressed his appreciation.

That next day, Katrina and I set out to walk with Tom up to the statue of Jesus on the hill. Along the way, we shared many ideas of the universal nature of spirituality to seek peace with the great unknown. It was a wonderful blessing to find so many similarities in our quest for understanding.

The day after that, the three of us went surfing together. The waves were much rougher the second time, but we continued to enjoy what seemed to be very deep conversations of universal spirituality and its applications in our lives. One of these conversations was overheard and then joined by a woman named Sara.

My experiences with Tom were some of my greatest joys during this month. It was an incredible reminder that we are all the same, regardless of how we try to fathom existence beyond our reasoning. Thank you, Tom, for sharing a part of your journey with me.

THE LONG ROAD HOME

Unexpected Greeting

Our team was wandering relatively aimlessly in the street, while trying to decide where to eat. As we stood there, a man walked up behind us and greeted us familiarly. It was Tom. He approached the team and this was the first time he had met them; he came out to eat with us the next night. Allison opened our meal with a prayer.

Tom told us this was the first time he had ever prayed over a meal. Katrina and I took the next day to show him the way to Jesus' statue at the top of the hill. We enjoyed our time together.

"It's amazing how much we have in common and that we happen to be visiting the same country at the same time," I mentioned.

"Indeed," he replied. "If I were a religious person, I would say it was meant to be."

Sara

Our first interaction with Sara was talking together on the beach. She replied to someone's question of the time with, "Just be here now." Katrina complimented her on this philosophy and then complimented Sara's tattoo that says the same. This opened the door for her to a universal spirituality conversation we were having with Tom.

After Katrina and I each expressed our viewpoints, Sara said she found them interesting and invited us to a barbecue her hostel was putting together the next day. We replied that we could stop by after church. Her face expressed shock. She said sarcastically, "That's fun." I explained that we were missionaries doing an 11 countries in 11 months journey.

She appeared surprised that we were missionaries and began to ask us about our personal beliefs. After we replied, she said it was refreshing to hear of churchgoers that were more accepting than the previous interactions she'd had. We were glad to hear that also and said our goodbyes. We said we'd enjoyed the conversation and would try to make it to the barbecue. She said she hopes to see us there. "I want more of this," were her last words to us that day.

The next day, Ryan and I went to touch base in the early afternoon and the grilling hadn't started yet. Katrina and I went back later that evening. Sara greeted us warmly and welcomed us graciously into her circle of hostel friends. We drank and played together for some time as though we'd known each other for years. I mentioned that I wanted to go visit my friend Tom's hostel because he was leaving the next day.

Sara came with us and shared with us a wondrous amount of her journey that had led her to the current point in her life. As we arrived at Tom's hostel we were told he'd gone to a barbecue. We opted to wait for him since he had likely been looking for us.

As we continued our discussion, Sara made a comment that was the highlight of both Katrina and my day. Sara said that she felt more at ease with us than even people in her hostel; she felt she could express herself with fewer filters with us than most people she'd known. She went on to say that coming out with us was the first time she'd left her hostel to go out and have fun, other than with other people from her hostel. We thanked her for the compliments, of both her words and her level of trust.

As time drew on, we gave up on waiting for Tom to return. We began the walk back to Sara's hostel. Along the way, we heard music coming out of one of the buildings. We checked it out and it was a dance club. We all decided to go inside. Sara danced, Katrina danced, and I danced. We all danced together.

We continued the rest of the way to her hostel together. We thanked her for inviting us to the barbecue and for coming out with us. She thanked us for sharing the evening with her. She gave us her Facebook tag and a hug, and then we went our separate ways.

My experiences with Sara were a reminder that too often we seek to change the people we encounter. This experience and the wonderful compliment of her feeling at ease with us, so much more so than with other Christians, reinforced a lesson that we must learn over and over again: **we are not called to condemn one another, but to live with and love one another.**

Thank you, Sara. Thank you for reminding us to simply be present wherever and whenever we are. Thank you for allowing us to share, if in even just the smallest part, of your personal journey.

Favorite Moments in Nicaragua

1. Sharing Bible studies together for hours in coffee shops
2. Challenging the team's ideas of progressive relationships
3. Seeing our team stick together through difficult feedback
4. Impromptu worship and night swimming in the ocean
5. Worshipping on the beach and singing in the streets
6. All night vigil with praying, walking, singing, and sunrise

Costa Rica

Summary

We spent one week between Nicaragua and Panama in Costa Rica. This was the second debrief of the Race for us. During this debrief we discussed what we had liked about our original teams, as well as what ways we would like to see each other continue to grow.

Then our new teams were selected for us.

Treasure Hunting

Our immediate reaction to the opportunity we had been given with the Ask the Lord month was excitement. This was in no small part because we would now have the space necessary to practice something we had been introduced to in Honduras. Ashley had shown us a video of a film crew that had gone "treasure hunting". This means that they simply prayed to the Lord for guidance to a soul who needed to hear His gospel. They had prayed for specific signs or words that would point them to this person. The phenomenal part of what they did was that they immediately followed His leadings. Of course, this worked perfectly in the film.

From our first conversations in Honduras, we all agreed that since we had such space in our month in Nicaragua we would like to try the theory out for ourselves. From even before we arrived in Nicaragua, we prioritized this high on our to-do list.

It never happened.

Leah had been most adamant about wanting to do this and had brought it up a couple times during the month. During our last team time in Nicaragua, she expressed frustration and anger that, although we all said we wanted to do this, it had never been done. She conceded that since we were leaving for Costa Rica and inevitable team changes the next day, treasure hunting just would not happen.

Admittedly, our team had been distracted in many ways during Nicaragua. The other ideas we had originally come up with (prayer vigil, beach and street hymns, coffee shop Bible studies) had all been done. There had been time available. None of us could give Leah a succinct answer as to why we never did it.

Except that we were scared and hadn't even known it.

Our heads were filled with doubts:

"What if we don't get any signs?"

"What if the signs don't lead anywhere?"

"What if the others get more signs than me?"

"If this doesn't work, am I not in touch with the Spirit?"

"If this doesn't work, does it show He's not listening?"

"Even worse, would it make me question His existence?"

We shared these concerns with one another. We admitted our fears. Then we resolved to test them. Even though the entire week in Costa Rica would be about transitioning us from one team to another, we could spend our free time following this one mission that we felt had slipped away from us. Tamarindo, Costa Rica would provide a perfect setting for us to do this. None of us had ever been there before.

Our team arrived in Tamarindo a day before the rest of the teams. We went to sleep. Then we woke and had a brief breakfast there in our hostel. As planned, we did not leave our hostel before starting our "treasure hunt."

As we sat together, Leah asked the Spirit to come and speak to us. We began to engage in listening prayer. We sat there quietly for about fifteen minutes. Then, as we slowly opened our eyes to one another, we shared specific words and visions we received. We all thought we were crazy. Brenna wrote down each of the words and visions we shared. *Railroad tracks with a diagonal line through them, a girl with super bright red hair "like fire", triangle, rectangle, a family, a very descript coffee mug, the sensation of wading in waves, books...*

Leah asked once again for the Holy Spirit to speak to us with specific signs to a person who needed to hear His Word. Another ten minutes went by in silence. We again shared the visions and words we thought were revealed to us. Brenna jotted them down again. *A diamond ring, teens arguing with parents, a trident, a fancy jeweled necklace, a child's hand burying itself in the sand, a toucan-looking bird, girl dancing on the beach, the giant word "WAR"...*

"Well, I guess let's go find 'em," someone said.

We left our hostel, entering into a city we had never stepped foot in before. Leaving our hostel, we turned right. We walked down a street that none of us were familiar with. As we turned the corner onto another street, there was a storm drain beneath us. It was made up of planks bolted into the concrete with small gaps between each plank. It was commented that they resembled *railroad tracks*. We all smiled, knowing we were stretching it a little. Then, as we walked in front of a hotel, the planks had a *diagonal stripe* across them indicating no parking.

Across the street from the hotel, we saw a coffee shop. "There must be coffee mugs in there," we thought. So we crossed the street to check. None of the mugs they had were quite the vision that had been shared so descriptively. However, in the shopping center next to the coffee shop was a store that we could not have seen from the other side of the street. It was a used bookstore with countless *books* in its storefront window.

The bookstore was closed, but we had a few avid readers on our team. We walked over to glance over their selection through the glass. After filling our hearts' desires for perusing the stock, we turned to head back towards the street. We walked past a few more shops before someone in the back of our party said, "Stop!" Those of us who had walked on, came back to see what she was pointing out. On the poster of a salon we had walked by was an advertisement for hair coloring. The girl on the poster had *bright red hair with flames* in the background.

We were all very excited! Many of us said that we were happy already that the experiment had worked as well as it had. It had already gone better than most of us expected. Our team continued down the road now with a new fervor. Along the way, we came across a *triangular* Yield sign. The next sign was *rectangular*.

"Okay, don't go stretching it too far," we thought.

The next sign was an advertisement for a nearby resort and restaurant. Its logo was a giant *trident*. We must have been on the right path. The road continued on for a while. Leah shared with us that she felt the important part of this experience was not the treasure, but rather the hunt. We decided to turn towards the sound of the ocean. We crossed between some buildings and wandered through some wooded area.

"We must be getting close."

The trees cleared to reveal the sands of the beach. Out in the distance, there could be seen one little boy building a sand castle. Just as we came walking out of the trees, he *buried his hand in the sand.*

We began to make our way toward him. Our view began to reach beyond the trees to the left and right. Behind a grouping of trees, we saw a few young teenagers playing together. Then their parents came into view sitting lazily on the beach. They made a cute *family*.

The little boy had now stopped playing in the sand. He'd run off into the shallow waves to be with his mother and father. Our team was now standing on the beach. We thanked God for His blessings that day. Watching the two separate families playing on the beach and in the waves, we wondered if our hunt had come to a close. We considered where to go next. It was argued that we would be disturbing the family on the beach and the little boy now seemed out of reach, since none of us had brought swimsuits of any kind.

Brenna still had the notebook she wrote our clues down on. I ask her to remind me of some of the clues we were searching for. I stripped down to my shorts. Then I waded out into the water. The *sensation of wading in waves* was refreshing. The little boy, his father, and mother were the only people in the water, so as I make my way toward them it is very apparent that I wanted to speak with them. The mother walked up to address me.

I explained to her that our team was a group of missionaries doing a "treasure hunt". I said that seeing a child's hand in the sand had been one of our clues, so we felt it important to seek their help. After I described some of the other clues we were still searching for, she told me that there was a restaurant a little way up the beach. This could lead us to the coffee mug we were looking for. Of the clues I had given her, she said this is the only one she would have any idea of how to find. I thanked her for her help. She wished us good luck on our search.

Just before I turn back toward the sand, I noticed her *fancy jeweled necklace*. I was surprised she was wearing it out into the water. I complimented her on it. She said, "Thank you," before turning back to her husband and son. I waded back up to the beach and shared the information she'd given me with my team.

We followed the lady's kind instructions toward a local restaurant that was just off the beach. On the plated glass door to the restaurant was a bird, but not quite the one we were looking for. As a group we decided to go on toward the street.

As we were walking on the side street, Allison spotted a lady coming out of the hotel across the street. The woman had on a *giant diamond ring*. Brenna and I crossed the street to strike up a conversation. The rest of the team followed. Allison explained in Spanish that we were missionaries, what we were doing, and some of the clues we had left to find. She also asked if we could pray for the woman in some way. The woman joyfully obliged us. She described having a *teenager* at home that struggled with drugs and *argues regularly with her*. We took turns praying for her and Allison closed the prayer in Spanish. The woman expressed what a blessing it was to have run into us on the short walk she had to the bus stop. The bus stop was just up the street from where we met her. Had we walked that street five minutes earlier or later, we never would have met her.

We continued on down the street a little way before exuberantly basking in God's faithfulness. Ryan suggested that the woman was the "treasure" we were meant to find. We all agreed fervently and decided it was time to thank God right then, right there. Circling up, we put our arms around each other.

"What kind of prayer should we do?"

"Should we go around the circle or warrior-style it?"

"*WAR!*" we all shouted!

Warrior style is a type of prayer that many of us had been introduced to at training camp. It is a style of prayer where everyone prays all at once, making a resounding cry to the Heavens. We prayed aloud right there in the middle of the street, circled up together, thanking God that not only had he heard us, but He had answered in a way that none of us had imagined.

We started making our way back to the hostel, still seeking some of the missing clues. There were some we never found.

Nonetheless, about two-thirds of our clues had led us directly to the woman who needed a little Spirit shared with her that day.

On our way back, we stopped as we considered whether to continue searching or call it a day. I wandered a little from the group toward the beach. A girl was there doing yoga; she looked like *she was dancing on the beach*. I shared with the team that I believe that all of the clues weren't meant to be found. It is a reminder that the hunt always continues.

Team Tear #6 – Brenna

Brenna had written a response to a squad leader coming to be with our team during the last month of Ask The Lord in Nicaragua. The whole team had been irritated that a squad leader was sent to oversee us for the last week of the only month we'd been free to seek ministry opportunities on our own. The squad leader had expectedly done an individual interview with each of us the first day of her arrival. Apparently Brenna had a great deal of reactions that had been withheld during that interview process.

She shared these with me the following week at our debrief.

As she spoke her eyes first became damp, then outright began to pour tears over her cheeks. She spoke of being hurt by condescending compliments for growth, faith, and confidence. She expressed rage that she had not released at others and herself for years. She passionately decried flaws in systems we had been dealing with for four months.

There with her tears, convictions, and valid criticisms, Brenna blossomed into someone previously unknown to us. She had stripped herself of naiveté. With a newfound faith in her own understanding, Brenna was trusting herself and walking in a confidence that can only be found from the Spirit within us.

"I have never been so proud of you," I told her. As we hugged one another, it felt like this was someone I'd never known before embracing me. I smiled and was looking forward to getting to know her.

Team Tear #7 – Ryan

At Subway in Tamarindo, as we walked into the store, I asked Ryan how he was doing with team changes. His eyes welled up and he said he'd been doing fine until we walked into Subway. Later in the night, as we were sharing our favorite moments with one another, I said seeing each of us give life to our new separate teams would be one of mine. I mentioned Ryan's ability to love and teach others the depths of love will be a blessing to his new teammates. He clenched my hand (we were all holding hands at that point) tightly as he held back his tears. Tears were in everyone's eyes as we each said goodbye to our original team.

Favorite Moments in Costa Rica

1. Treasure hunting
2. Being so proud of Leah becoming team leader, Brenna embracing her continued role as logistics coordinator, and Allison accepting her invitation to be squad leader
3. Teaching Missy to surf
4. Seeing surfers and their teachers complimenting our surfing
5. Surfing in on the last wave together
6. Hearing Amanda say she's excited for Leah to lead us & wanting to support her

Panama

Summary

Our new team (Hola Ola) experienced a very eclectic ministry in Panama. There was no routine schedule, but we were provided an outlined schedule of what the different days would be filled with during our month.

Before we would receive this, we were given an opportunity to venture with a team from YWAM (Youth With A Mission) out into the Darién Gap. For those who do not know (just as I did not before taking our adventure), the Darién Gap is basically a no-man's land between Panama and Colombia. It is a stretch of land that has no road connecting the two countries. This is because the jungle and swamp are so thick that building a road through the territory is considered too costly, both financially and environmentally. Indigenous tribes make up the primary population and they are sparsely spread out throughout the region.

Our journey began with a four and a half hour car ride on a single paved road through two border crossing checkpoints. These checkpoints were certainly a unique experience because they neither really marked an exit from Panama, nor did they mark an entrance into Colombia. Although still north of the official border, for all practical purposes, we were considered outside of both countries.

Many may have a hard time imagining what this means. Suffice it to say that the only support we would receive in any way would be that, at the second border crossing, they checked all of our passports, noted how many of us there were and asked when we expected to return. This seemed standard questioning to me. It became a little more significant when our host explained why those particular questions were asked. If we did not come back out when we were expecting to or if there were fewer members than went in, then they would send military in to find us with the assumption something has gone wrong. With that, they wished us luck and waved us through.

As we turned off of the paved road, our two vehicle caravan trudged along an unpaved dirt path through the trees for about an hour and a half. The path comes to a stop when it reaches the river. We unpack all of our necessary equipment and load up two canoes with motors on the back. These canoes take us fifteen minutes upstream and then we walk the last ten minutes from the river, with all of our equipment in hand.

This brought us to a hidden village that has close to five hundred residents. From the top of the hill you can see each and every little home that makes up the village. Beyond that, trees. A three hundred and sixty degree view of nothing but jungle for as far as the eye can see in every direction.

Service

We spend three days with the Embéra tribe. The first day we walk door-to-door introducing ourselves and asking families if we can pray for them. Almost all welcome us with smiles and thank us for praying over their personal concerns. After lunch our itinerary is disclosed to us. We will use a projector that our host brought with him to provide a movie night for the village. After lunch we take three different directions and work in teams picking up garbage throughout the village. To our joy, many little children join us, excited to be a part of the project!

We return to many of the homes we visited earlier in the day in order to invite them to join us for the movie. One woman, in turn, invites us to join her for church the following evening. As the evening approaches, we run into a problem with the projector. Since a significant number of villagers have already told us they will come, I ask our host what Plan B is. "I'm open to suggestions," he replies. I pause for a moment, waiting for a laugh. Nope. He is serious.

I look around and think about all of my teammates' natural abilities. I interrupt Amanda as she is playing the guitar for some children nearby.

"Can you play some songs for a worship service?"
"I can pull some together," she assures me.

Justin responds that he would be willing to narrate our service, as a sort of Master of Ceremonies. Claire tells me she can read a Bible verse. I can put together a lesson for them. Missy can play games with kids. Leah quickly volunteers to sit in the audience with the children, to help keep them engaged. (For anyone who has never worked with children and plans to, this is an absolute must. Adults sitting with children to show that it is fun to be fully *participative and cooperative is a <u>highly</u> underrated, necessary component of any kids' program.)*

I am excited and proud of our team for being ready, willing, and able at the drop of a hat! I tell our host we have a worship service ready for the village! "Well, we got the projector working now," he tells me. So... we watch The Lion, The Witch, and The Wardrobe *with everyone that evening.*

The next day, the girls on our team identify a great opportunity that is not built into our service schedule. We are spending our time in the Darién Gap jointly with a team from YWAM (Youth With A Mission). They are a little younger and relatively new to the mission field. They have just completed a three-month training but are only a few weeks into the service aspect of the program. At the recommendation of the ladies on our team, we take a brief time to simply engage listening prayer and then speak the encouraging messages we believe they need to hear. I am again proud of my team as I witness each and every one of them speak life into these new beacons who are joining the field.

This would mark the first experience I have with a lesson repeated to me over and over again throughout the remaining time on the race. **Life Lesson: It is just as important to share love with your team, as it is to share love with the communities you serve together.**

That afternoon, a few members of the YWAM team presented a penny stove to the village. They demonstrated how to make a compact working stove with soda cans, a knife, a penny, and a little bit of lighter fluid. This proved to be a very popular presentation, especially for the ladies who sold lighter fluid and sodas in their shops!

Following this, two of the other YWAMers and myself spent the afternoon playing basketball with the local village men. They thanked me for what our team had said to them and appreciated a little more confidence as they moved forward with their mission.

The second evening we had an opportunity to visit the local church we had been invited to. Leah, Amanda, myself, and a YWAMer named Jessie visited the local service. We were there an hour early because we had misunderstood our invitation. Jessie began playing the piano while we waited and, to her surprise, was asked to continue playing as the congregation arrived! Then, the pastor asked her if she would like to play the music in the first few songs of the service! It was a beautiful expression of harmonic synchronicity between our two cultures. This was truly an organic experience of two love cultures simply embracing each other's gifts.

After the church service we enjoyed coffee with the congregation and the pastor. We said our goodbyes and then returned to our team. This evening is free, so I had asked if we could provide the worship service for the village anyway. Our host was excited to let us take the opportunity. We had again extended invites by word of mouth throughout the village. When the time came for us to start the worship service, we had very few people arrive to join us. Admittedly, our team was a little disappointed and debated whether we should even go through with our program. But as the hour went by, more and more children came to be a part of the event. Soon, we had easily somewhere between fifty and one hundred children playing the games we used to fill time.

We decided it was time. Missy helped herd the children into a crowd and sat them down. Justin introduced the evening with prayer. Amanda played a few songs for them. Claire read the scripture of the Good Samaritan. I followed the scripture with an interactive skit, identifying the values of caring for one another. Throughout the whole time, I witnessed Leah actively seeking out children who seemed disinterested and helped them to join the activities. We closed with a few more songs, and then shut the evening down with one more prayer.

This was one of my favorite moments with Hola Ola.

It also proved to be an important lesson for the YWAM team. The next day, we all packed up our things, said our goodbyes to the village, and set off to return back into Panamanian cityscape. Along the way, separate team members of YWAM told separate teammates of ours that they had a meeting immediately after that worship service. They told us that seeing unity among us inspired them to try to enact more with themselves. The Lord always has plans for us that we can never know.

The rest of our time in Panama presented us with a wide variety of ministry experiences. These included:
- *building a septic tank for a poor family*
- *visiting schools to talk about environmental conservation*
- *preparing and presenting a full-day children's worship program*
- *participating in a city soccer tournament*
- *beginning a barrel-ponics fish hatchery system*
- *repainting the interior of a home*
- *translating for visiting missionaries' presentations*
- *lining the base of a fence with a concrete foundation*
- *visiting with other missionaries based in the country*

Unexpected Greeting

A girl called out "Patricio!" and waved from the *tienda* (store) while our team was walking to the bus stop in the morning. This *tienda* was across from a school and a church. After a few repeat glances, her face and voice became familiar to us. She had been in the kids' program we had put together at the church the previous weekend.

Leadership Development Workshop

During prayer one morning, I had an expectation that Amanda and Leah would have a great journey seeking our new hostel for this month's conference. I pictured them meeting a young man that will surprise them by speaking English. When I shared this with Leah before they left, she said she had the same idea.

Amanda called me during the next day to say that their day had been a wonderful joy and that a young man's incredible English had surprised them. They had found us a hostel for that next weekend's retreat.

Favorite Moments in Panama

1. Encouraging the YWAM team together
2. Doing the impromptu kids' service in El Salto; going to and being in El Salto
3. Longer, deeper talks with Justin
4. Putting together and doing the kids' service in Panama; seeing everyone pull together
5. Going to the Panama Canal as a team
6. Having dinner with Ken and Elena

Colombia

Summary

Sacrifice.

The first week we were in Colombia, this was the most important lesson God put on my heart. As I lay in my bed, I knew my team was out enjoying a championship soccer game. In Latin America, this is an experience that engages the culture like no other. I was afraid that I would not have an opportunity like this again.

I was right.

Nevertheless, even though the opportunity to go with them had been presented to me, I would remain there in my bunk. Men actively participating in the rehabilitation program were not allowed to go out on excursions. Neither would I for the week I was enrolled.

I woke with the men in the program. I worked with the men in the program. I ate with the men in the program. I prayed with the men in the program. I grew with them.

***

On the second day of our arrival, we were asked by our contact how comfortable we were sharing different parts of our lives in ministry. I asked if I could join the men and enroll in the program for a week. Our host was ecstatic to give me the opportunity and I joined the next day. For seven days, I was no different than any other participant in the program. This was, at the same time, both one of the best and worst decisions I made throughout the entire Race.

My time with the men opened many opportunities that simply would not have existed had I not been willing to put my life into theirs in such a way. There were times that I would be approached outside of scheduled activities for advice, for counsel, for camaraderie. Particular men in the program that other leaders had problems with worked willingly with me, both while having discussions and while doing cooperative projects. I saw hard men lower their guard and soft men raise their resolve. **I am grateful for every moment I shared in the program.**

My time away from my team could never be repaired. There were times that divisions were felt among us. There were times that we felt alone with each other by our sides. There was faith lost and hope diminished. The ministry's division of genders isolated the only other man on my team for that week I was away. The women of our team would struggle to work together as they experienced new dynamics without us. **I am sorry for every moment I missed from my team.**

A lesson I learned without realizing it.
Sacrifice.

Service

The majority of our work was directly with the rehabilitation program. We conducted Bible study devotionals, participated in prayer times, provided sermon messages, and simple encouragement to individuals recovering from any number of self-destructive habits.

Additionally, we were very active in the children's Vacation Bible School. We walked the blocks delivering invitations to the local neighborhoods. We performed a skit each morning illustrating the creation story. We provided games and aided the teachers during their lesson times. Each day, we even walked the children home after the program concluded.

A substantial weekly outreach that we participated in was a feeding program out in the streets. Volunteers from the program would take bread and tinto (coffee with sugar) in a truck to the largest shantytown in Medellin. This is a populous living under a bridge that is made up of hundreds of active drug users. There is no catch. No one had to proclaim Jesus as their savior or renounce their drug use. In fact, most everyone we served was high when we served them their bread. This had simply been the first outreach of Ciudad Refugio and it continues to this day. It was hard for some of us to see such hopelessness, but it was a blessing to be part of a program bringing life to the dying.

- *Additional opportunities we worked with this month included:*
- *helping with a "home-school" program that taught the kids of the volunteers or program participants*
- *singing in worship services*
- *aiding in the nightly homeless shelter run by the program*

- *delivering recycled products to fundraise the program*
- *taking the women in the program for a "night-out"*
- *providing Sunday School lessons for children*
- *childcare during adult worship services*

Richard*

After my first introduction to the men in the program of Ciudad De Refugio in Colombia, a young man came up and introduced himself in English. He said his name was Richard and explained he'd been in America for 19 years before coming to Colombia. He said he normally got in trouble for talking too much, but felt that it was alright to come talk to me at the time. We formed a quick bond. He mentioned he'd been incarcerated in Texas for a good portion of his time in America and I told him my dad was there now.

I made it a point to encourage him when I could over the next few days. The next Thursday morning, I witnessed him almost come to blows with another guy before the daily 6:30 a.m. prayer time. I sat next to him and asked him what had happened. He explained that the two of them were supposed to clean the shower stalls and toilets together. The other guy accused him of not doing his part. He calmly denied it, but the other guy raised his voice saying he didn't like the way Richard kept to himself all the time. Richard complained that he wasn't being spoken to with respect. The other guy, Frank*, said if they'd met outside the program he'd tear him apart. They bowed up to each other but neither threw a punch.

Richard went on to say that he was just gonna have to show Frank later on the soccer field how men deal with their problems. At this time, the prayer time began. I sat silently next to Richard for a few minutes before beginning to pray for him. I prayed aloud so I was sure he would hear me. I prayed a prayer of thanks for Richard's strength and the grace in his life. I prayed that he would know this day that he did not need to rely on his own strength, but that he could rely on the strength of God's Spirit. I prayed that his life could change this day and that he only needed to rely on a strength outside his own to see how life could be so different. I prayed peace over him, a peace that shows no concern for who pushes nor prods him in any way. I thanked God for hearing my prayer.

As I had been praying, Richard had begun to weep. With tears streaming down his cheeks and snot dripping over his mouth, he began to pray for himself. I only heard two words: beautiful and *dificil* (difficult). But I could tell that he was fervently trying to change his heart by the way his hands clenched into fists and his arms shook with unspoken emotion. After a while, his breathing slowed and his arms relaxed. The prayer time came to a close. I quickly put my arms over his shoulder and told him I was proud of him for making the change. I told him he would come to know a peace he had never known before. I told him that there is a Spirit in him now that shows no concern for contempt and I thanked the Spirit for coming upon him. He turned to smile and he thanked me.

When the men all went out to play soccer that afternoon, I saw a few guys talking with Frank. He pointed at Richard with intent; Richard noticed but paid it no mind. He hadn't even dressed to play. No fight occurred that day with these men. Richard spent the afternoon sitting on the sideline chatting happily with one of the volunteer leaders. I put an arm around his shoulder as we walked away from the soccer field and told him I was proud of him.

"The Spirit is stronger than we know," he replied.

He went on to tell me that Frank got into a confrontation that did not lead to blows with someone else later that day. The other guy had opted to go home. Richard said the devil was out to get someone out of the program that day. He said with confidence and gratitude that it hadn't been him.

*These names have been changed out of respect for these men's privacy.

What Pictures Could Never Show

Lying in an empty bed, I decided I would share with everyone as much as I can about my current journey. But pictures are not allowed in the inpatient drug rehabilitation program I have spent my last week enrolled in here in Colombia.

The primary reason for this rule is that many of the men in this program still have people looking for them. Whether it was a drug deal gone wrong, the inevitable end to gang conflicts, or simply their victims or victims' families looking for vengeance, these men's privacy, in many cases literally, is a matter of life and death. Broken families, broken lives, and broken hearts fill the air here in Medellin.

Hopelessness is the strongest aversion to growth and it is prominent in this place. Nevertheless, Fundacion Ciudad Refugio continues to provide a place where men can come to escape their addictions to drugs, alcohol, sex, gambling, violence, or any other vice that binds them in chains of self-deprecation.

I was nervous enrolling my first day. I would be submitting myself to the authority of the program for the next seven days. This was something new for me.

The rules are rigid:
- Follow the schedule from the time you wake up at 5:00 a.m. until lights out at 9:00 p.m.
- Meals must take no more than 10-15 minutes and no one is allowed to sit at the table.
- Buckets of water make up your showers, how you wash your clothes, and the way you flush the toilets.
- Chores include sweeping the street, mopping the six flights of stairs each day, taking care of the dog, and cleaning the bathrooms.
- Of the three prayer times each day, two of them must be

done standing or walking so that no one is falling asleep.
- Classes and lectures must be attended with proper attention to avoid receiving *disciplina* (discipline).

It is a strict program of discipline, but it proves necessary and is given in love for men who have spent their entire lives without any structure except where the next hit is coming from or who the gang is going to roll.

After a few days, I fell into the routine as a new normal. I began to see some of the fruit that the program bares. Not only do these men receive a foundation in their lives, but also they share it with others. Some of the more advanced members of the program operate the ministries of the foundation, including the discounted street bakery, the recycling program, and the shelter that provides a night's rest to 50-60 men 365 days a year.

On Saturday, the opportunity arose for me to share with the men in the program, and the homeless men who come to the shelter, a message in their weekly worship service. I shared with them my personal testimony. The men and my time in the program had changed me. I shared not only my personal testimony, but also all the gritty details along the way. As I shared with these men stories of violent anger and sexual immorality, I asked them to raise their hands if they had experienced similar situations. And as I expressed to them "*Yo tambien* (Me too)," I could see on their faces a more vested interest in what I was sharing. Throughout my story, a power came over me that I had not been prepared for. I described how the church and Spirit of God changed my life. I described how He wants to change their lives as well, if only they would be willing to let him. I asked who was tired of struggling to satisfy their own desires, only to find that it is a neverending pursuit. I was humbly in awe as two-thirds of the men in the program and one-third of the homeless men stepped up to the front.

Earlier in the day, I had prayed that God would reach into these men's hearts to change their lives and that I would simply be used to do it. By this time in my story, I was hardly forming the words. It felt more that I was hearing them, as though they were being shared with me as much as the audience itself. I was grateful to have the opportunity to pray for these men as we closed the service. I walked through the group of hardened gangsters, hopeless drug addicts, and wandering vagrants, touching each man's head or shoulder as I prayed for him. And as the tears rolled down their cheeks, I saw hearts soften, hope restored, and a new foundation built upon love. After the service came to a close I sat down, looked up, and thanked God for what I had just been a part of. Then I helped stack the chairs, break down the sound stage, and returned to my bunk with five other men.

Over the course of the next few days, I would have many opportunities to answer questions about how to deal with anger, how to control one's emotions, and how we must choose to face life in a new way. I am incredibly grateful for what these men have taught me through their experiences, interactions, and longing for understanding. As I exited the program, I asked them all to remember that they are destined for a greater purpose than drugs or other addictions would tell them. I thanked them for teaching me the same.

We are all designed to be greater than our bad habits. We must also remember we are designed to be greater than our good habits. When we sacrifice not part of our lives, but our lives in their entirety to the Spirit who longs to be our strength, then we will be rewarded with a new life, a life that is better than any we could picture for ourselves.

Unexpected Greeting

While Justin and I returned from buying a pizza for our first man night, a couple of guys carrying bags of food said hello to us on the street. As we walked closer to them, we could see it was two of the guys from the program. They were out walking the street because they were delivering a food order from the program's bakery.

Jamie*

During the last week I was in Colombia, I was asked one morning a series of questions I didn't understand. It was just before someone else's talk, so I said that we could talk afterward. Visibly irritated, Jamie said I didn't understand. He was right. *No entiendes* (you don't understand) were the only words I could decipher. As another volunteer gave the talk, I prayed that God would speak to Jamie through me. That the language barrier would disappear or that I would simply be able to bumble out something helpful for him that I could not understand.

After the talk, Jamie went back to his work in the workshop making coffee cup rings. I pursued him and asked if he wanted to talk. We stepped out onto the stairs and he explained that he had woke up tired, both physically and in his heart. He asked what to do or what the problem was. Lessons I'd shared with clients over many years came back to me and the words to explain them in Spanish coalesced in my mind. I explained that we all have down days. I explained that we all experience ups and down; they are a natural part of life. I said the devil lies to us, telling us that life should be smooth all the time. I said if we believe this lie, we will never experience great sufferings but we will also never experience great joys. I shared with him that when I experience those down days, I remember this lesson and am grateful that life will soon bring me equal joy to my sorrow.

As he smiled and looked off pensively, I could see he understood my meaning. He thanked me and shook my hand. Two days later, he pulled me aside when I saw him at worship service. He thanked me again and said he had woken up that second morning rejuvenated without any concrete reason. I thanked God for blessing him in this way and for teaching me anew this valuable lesson.

*This name has been changed out of respect for this man's privacy.

Team Tear #8 – Justin

Our team had been having a difficult time as we were close to finishing Colombia. We were still feeling out how to interact with one another six weeks after teams had been changed. There was an air of thickness that seemed to block our connections with one another. This culminated into our most necessary and difficult conversation as a team.

Leah had called a team time to share our greatest joys and challenges over the last few days. As usual at that time, everyone shared minimally and quickly anticipated the end of the meeting. But this time, something different happened. Karissa asked why there was such tension among us. At this point, honesty began to break through. Slowly, individual team members began to express unmentioned irritations and pet peeves.

As the circle came around to Justin, he questioned the purpose of this exercise. He admitted that he found it hard to accept a system of support that seemed to be lacking in the first six months of his race. As he went on, he explained that he had felt support from almost no one since the beginning of his time on the field.

Tears began to roll down his cheeks as he described an overwhelming loneliness experienced as far back as training camp. Finally expressing himself and stating plainly grievances never let loose before, we saw in Justin a softer side that had not been present previously.

His willingness to be vulnerable set a tone for the rest of our conversation. Three other team members joined in the tears and prayers were poured over one another. We still had work to do if we wanted to care for each other. But the process had finally begun.

Team Tear #9 – Amanda

Our most difficult and necessary conversation continued. Our time in Colombia had been hard on all of us and there was still ice in the air when we met for team times. It had been validly observed that the loving community we hoped for seemed to be lacking warmth. But as the conversation turned to individual feedback, the words became harsh.

Individual team members shared their griefs with each other one by one. The nails came out as attention turned toward Amanda. As a teammate unyieldingly attacked her personal character and individual faith, she appeared first to be shocked and then genuinely hurt. The accusation was made that she always abandoned difficult situations and the blame was falsely laid at her feet for the lack of community we were generally experiencing.

In a brave effort to connect, Amanda asked to pray for her persecutor. She was roughly refused by this teammate claiming they wanted nothing to do with her, in life or in prayer or in any other way. We were all at a loss for what should come next. With tears in her eyes, Amanda asked if she should leave. No response was given. She stood up to leave and walked out the door. For a moment, it seemed the accusation of her walking away in difficult situations would prove true. There would be no resolution.

Then she came bolting back in. The tears were even more prevalent, but now she had an enthusiastic energy behind them.

"You may not want me to pray for you, but I'm going to right now anyway."

No protest was made. She poured words of grace through her prayer and spoke love to someone who had just cast her as far away as possible. When she finished her prayer, eyes were raised to see tears in four more faces including the one being prayed over. Our spirits were broken and we were one body for the first time.

Her act of courageous love demonstrated that we can care for each other even in the face of absolute vindication. She reached out through her pain to the one who was hurting her and brought healing to them both. Amanda transcended her own struggles that day in order to bring love to a place filled with animosity. If we aspire to bring the Kingdom of Heaven to a world that knows nothing of compassion, we must aspire to break ourselves free in the same way.

We must be willing to demonstrate that those who persecute us are not our enemies, but simply our brothers and sisters who are longing for a love that only comes through miracles.

Luke*

Luke was a great companion to Justin and I during our time in Colombia. Luke was a graduate of the recovery program that made up our primary ministry. He continued to live there in the volunteers' dorms now and helped run the program.

He bunked with us throughout the whole month.

One of the last few days we were there, I was pulled aside and asked to keep an eye on him when we went out to minister to a local shantytown. I asked him if he wanted this also. He said that he did. He had been having problems controlling his emotions concerning girls.

We visited the shantytown and walked through the community of active drug use together. We purposely avoided speaking to women that may very well try to entice him in some way. We returned to our ministry site and went to make some coffee for our bunk. There was no coffee, so I offered to go get some at a nearby corner store. He opted to go with me.

As we walked the street, he explained to me that he was having a hard time following his own rules about interactions with women. The corner store we were looking for was closed, so we continued on to another one down the street. We picked up the coffee and sat down for a quick drink at a table outside the shop. On the television above us was a beautiful barely clothed woman.

"The devil is everywhere," he observed as he motioned towards the television. We moved to a different table.

He continued on to tell me that he just didn't know how he was supposed to act. He didn't know if he should maintain the rules he had setup for himself or if he should pursue these feelings or what. He looked down at the table without finding any resolution.

I prayed that God would give me wisdom to share with him. I have certainly had my own struggles with these same feelings! Without knowing where I was going to end up, I just started talking.

I told him that I had experienced the same struggle. He looked up at me with a little disbelief before letting his gaze fall down again. I elaborated to let him know that it had happened even on the Race. I explained to him that we had restrictive rules about mixed gender relations throughout our journey.

"That can be pretty difficult when you have four men traveling together with twenty women!" I exclaimed.

I told him about how on my first team I had become attracted to a teammate of mine. I admitted that we had talked about it and she had been attracted to me as well.

His face was watching mine now, looking for any possible sign of deception. There were none to be found.

We had shared with the organization that we had these feelings with the full expectation that they would split us up. They did.

I told him that I still have feelings for this girl, but I would wait until the time is right to pursue the relationship. God has a perfect timing planned that goes beyond our feelings, perceptions, or understanding.

"Thank you," he smiled. I could see he was working something out in his mind that he did not share with me.

Two days later, he was not in our bunk. It was the last weekend before we would move on to Ecuador. I asked our host if everything was okay. He told me everything was fine. Luke had simply decided that while there were twenty women waiting around for their travel day, he did not need to be there. He would return on Monday when our group moved on.

The last day we were there was a Sunday. I saw him sitting at the back of the congregation. I went over to sit by him and asked if everything was all right.

"Everything in God's time," he replied. Our bus left immediately after the service. I hugged him before I left.

"I'm proud of you," I let him know.

"*Gracias, hermano* (Thank you, brother)." He waved with a

smile as I walked toward the bus.

Favorite Moments in Colombia

1. Sharing my testimony with the men in the program
2. Encouraging the men as my program ended
3. Sharing my testimony and words of sacrifice/encouragement with Hola Ola
4. Riding the motorcycle back from the drug/homeless camp (El Rio) & in between a bus and a taxi
5. Going to see Jurassic World with Karissa and Marcela

6. Riding our roommate's motorcycle
7. Paragliding outing with Hola Ola
8. Hearing our teammate's admit their grievances with one another; seeing them laugh together afterwards

PATRICK BOOTH

Ecuador

Summary

Our first month with our second new team. This month was structured incredibly well by our host. More than having a routine schedule, we were actually given a written agenda for the whole month! (This rarely happens on the mission field.)

We stayed with a ministry called IncaLink, whose primary purpose is to house incoming short-term mission teams. "What a nightmare!" I thought to myself. I could not imagine having to spend the bulk of my time providing hospitality for people who want to visit the mission field briefly and then go back to their comfortable lives with "war stories" about how rough it was wherever they spent this minimal time. (Don't worry. I realized how self-righteous this thought was later. This was a lesson I would learn in Ecuador and then again in Peru.) They made our experience so comfortable. It was easily the most pleasant accommodations we had throughout the entirety of our race. They take their ministry very seriously and they are excellent at it!

During our stay with IncaLink, we had opportunities to spend time with weeklong mission teams. This provided a new experience for us because for the first time on our race, we were the veterans. These teams looked to us for guidance. They looked to us for direction. It was an unexpected joy to be able to provide it for them, simply by doing what we do everyday while on the field... albeit a little bit slower, so that they could follow our lead.

Life Lesson: There is just as much value providing a connection for others as there is in making the connection yourself.

Parent Vision Trip

This month also was the month that our parents were able to come visit us for a brief time. I was presented with a unique opportunity because of this. Our team was in the city that the Parent Vision Trip would be held at. Adventures in Missions had allotted three days of travel time between ministry schedules and the beginning of the PVT for other teams to travel to our city. This gave our team three days with no agenda, since we had no traveling to do.

I asked my mother if she would like to come early, in order to visit the Galapagos Islands with me. She immediately responded with an enthusiastic yes, so we visited the islands for three days prior to the week all of us would spend together. This was one of the most joyful experiences I had on the race! It was an incredible blessing to be able to share such a special time with the woman that shaped me to be who I am today.

Furthermore, it was a joy to freely spend the rest of the time sharing experiences with other racers and their parents. We had spent six months getting to know one another, but now we were able to see each other in a brand new way. No matter how much anyone denies it, everyone acts a little different with their parents around.

Service

During the first few weeks of our time in Ecuador, we helped build a house for an impoverished family. The weekly lunch program that was our primary ministry staffed an active social worker to assess the needs of the families coming to receive lunches. They then try to meet the needs in any way they can. The family we helped to build a house for had three families living in two rooms. It was a great service opportunity to improve the living conditions of all the families involved, but God seemed to have a more profound purpose prepared.

It was a great blessing to be able to improve their lives practically by aiding in the building project, but our real calling was revealed to us as the project progressed. Through unexpected common interests and mutual hobbies, we formed a bond with this family that went deeper than any of us imagined when the project began. This common ground we found demonstrated to our team that we were helping not just an anonymous recipient, but a family much like our own. The reciprocal experiences we shared demonstrated to the family that they were not only recipients of loving compassion, but had every capability of providing their own value as well.

Life Lesson: The human connection that is shared with recipients provides both a sense of compassion from the missionary and a recognition of personal value (self-worth) from the beneficiary. This is arguably the most important aspect of all missions.

***

After we completed the building project, we focused our attention on a weeklong soccer camp for youth. We packed lunches for them, provided daily devotionals and songs, played games, organized exercises, officiated competitions, as well as walked the children to and from the parks each day.

The Parent Vision Trip proceeded after our time with the soccer camp. While our parents were with us we aided the weekly lunch program, participated in the closing days of a nearby Vacation Bible School, and spent time with family rejuvenating our spirits for the remainder of the race.

Being Jesus

"Christian" was originally a derogatory term for a small Jewish sect that followed the teachings of Jesus Christ. The church adopted this term and classifies all people who profess their belief in Christ as members. But being like Jesus doesn't always appear the way we imagine it should.

My first lesson in this came at the end of my time in Colombia. Our team had been asked to portray the creation story in a drama for a children's Vacation Bible School. Unknowingly, I had been volunteered by my team to play the part of Jesus. I happily adopted the role and enjoyed sharing with children the story of God creating the earth, skies, plants, animals, and finally Adam and Eve. We concluded the drama on a Friday to prepare for our 20-hour bus ride on Saturday night. Unexpectedly, they told us Friday that they would like to share the drama with another group of children in the park on Saturday. We'd been given Saturday off so that we could rest and prepare for our long journey that evening.

I knew that they would honor their agreement to let us rest on Saturday, but I could not imagine making them recast the drama at the last minute. I volunteered to pack my bags Friday night and rest while on the bus. It occurred to me then that being Jesus doesn't have a time clock and doesn't end when our ministry schedule says we are finished. Sharing the creation and gospel story with the children in the park was one of my most memorable experiences in Medellin.

***

The lesson was driven home through a most joyful experience during my first few weeks in Ecuador. We spent the first week of the month building a house for an impoverished family. The first few days we were there, we interacted with the family very little. My group and I and the family simply followed the instructions of the foreman, putting the house together from the foundation piece by piece.

As we continued to work with them while the foreman was called to head other jobs, however, something changed. We began to work less and speak more. They began to work more and to speak more. Missy discovered that the husband we are building for, Nelson, and myself share a mutual hobby: watching professional wrestling. We shared many discussions about who is past their prime in the sport and which rookies will have skills for years to come. They began to cook for us each day we came to work on the house. We would all sit down to lunch while Nelson shared videos of recent wrestling events that I hadn't been able to watch because I'd been on the mission field. He said this was the first time any team coming to help them had come inside their home to watch videos or to eat with them.

I told them I carried wrestling masks with me and they asked each day for me to bring them to the work site. One Thursday, I did just that. They all had a field day of taking pictures with the masks on them, their children, pretending to battle each other with them! I could see the incredible amount of joy it brought into their lives. At the end of the day, I gifted the masks to Nelson and his younger brother. With tears streaming down his face, Nelson said that many people had helped them with gifts in the past, but this was very special. He received them graciously and insisted we are part of his family. Four other brothers spoke of the encouragement they were glad to see their brother receive in a way they had never seen before. As they wiped a few tears from their eyes, they thanked us and blessed our continued journey.

By the end of the project, we'd spent days talking about wrestling, a half of a workday dancing, and many afternoons eating. Nelson and his brothers took more ownership and pride in their work each day we shared with them. In the last few days, they worked with smiles on their faces while asking us for conversation only.

We came to build a house of cinder blocks and concrete. But God used our unexpected common interests to build a foundation of His Spirit: a spirit of love, excitement, compassion, and understanding that will live in the hearts of His children long after the cinder has returned to dust.

Unexpected Greeting

As Justin and I were waiting to cross the street heading towards our ministry site, we heard a soft little girl's voice call out *"Patricio!"* We turned to see the young child come out from the bus stop. She ran right up to give me a hug. Her mom smiled before they walked off together. It had been one of the sweet children attending the soccer camp.

Favorite Moments in Ecuador

1. Pulling roses out of the trash and giving them to the girls
2. Mitad del Mundo with Claire, Missy, and the Canadians
3. Watching wrestling with the family served
4. Giving my masks away to the family
5. Watching Into the Woods with Claire
6. Watching Jurassic World with Allison
7. Dancing with Missy, Allison, Claire, Dani, and Nicole at dinner
8. Closing prayer for the squad at PVT
9. Eating with Dar Vida and our parents in Quito
10. Seeing "treasure hunting" incorporated into PVT

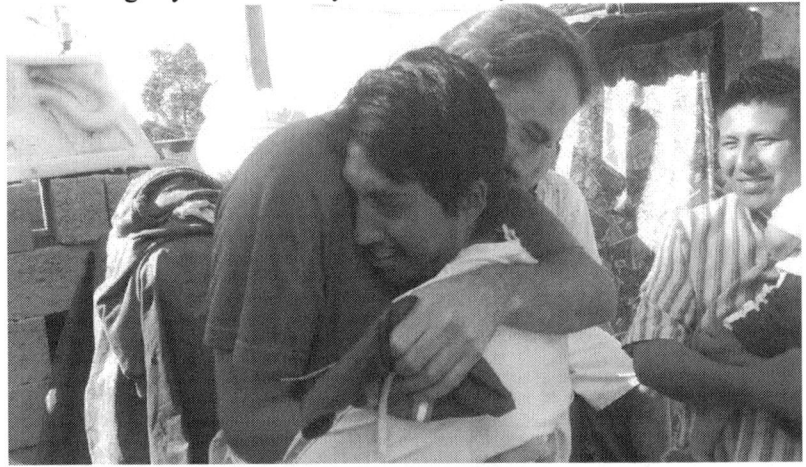

Each of us were asked to share a story of how the Race had effected us with our parents. I shared the "treasure hunting" story. I explained that I had been Christian my whole life and had always believed in God. The "treasure hunting" experience gave me a new belief not just in God, but also in God's miracles. During one of our ministry days at Pan de Vida, we ran into a problem of having too many volunteers. We were then informed that we would

be broken up into groups and would go "treasure hunting." It was a joy to see that it had been unexpectedly incorporated. Moreover, it was incredible to share the experience with our parents!

PATRICK BOOTH

Peru

Summary

There is no way to summarize the experiences had during our month in Peru. Our ministry was eclectic and our excursions were extraordinary. We were hosted once again by IncaLink, except that this time we would serve with them as our primary ministry as well. IncaLink had two short-term teams with them when we arrived and we enjoyed their company for the brief time we had together. They remained there with us for only the first four or five days. Even stranger, the mission coordinators that had hosted their teams' experiences also left along with the short-term teams. This left us with no mission coordinators or teams in a ministry whose primary purpose is to host incoming mission teams.

Luckily for us, there is a wide range of ongoing mission projects that IncaLink conducts on its own. Truthfully, we felt a little left behind after the short-term teams left. The ongoing mission projects had been briefly described to us and we were told we would have the option to participate in any of these, but we had not been instructed on how this would happen. After a week that felt like we were simply participating in whatever ministry happened to cross our path, our team leader suggested we identify a particular ministry to work with purposefully. This was very helpful to us because there had been so many options it was hard for us to focus our efforts in any one area. After we each selected a ministry it was easier to identify individual purposes and prioritize who would focus on which projects, especially since many of them would have service opportunities simultaneously.

Beyond the service opportunities came an opportunity that is only available one place in the entire world. Visit Machu Picchu. I knew that I wanted to visit this as soon as I found out we were spending a month in Peru. Much to my dismay, we were still very far from the historic site. However, our team leader and another team member of mine also wanted to visit the site. So we asked for some leniency on our schedule from our host, who was just as excited as we were that we would be able to visit it. We started researching how to get there on our weekly outings to the mall, which provided our only Internet access. After the second weekend of this, we were able to include four members from another team as well. They really put together most of the arrangements for us and from then on, we simply followed their instructions.

On my birthday, we enjoyed a delicious meal together at the base village that rests beneath Machu Picchu. The next morning we went up the mountain and spent all day exploring the ruins. It was one of my favorite excursions of the year. Unexpectedly, one of the finest points in the day was simply lying in the grass with the sun shining down on my face. I slipped in and out of sleep in the middle of the afternoon. This was one of the most peaceful experiences I have ever had.

Since we had flown separately to Cusco in order to visit Machu Picchu, we continued to enjoy leisure time for a few days while waiting for the rest of our squad to meet us at the border. This allowed us time to visit Los Uros, the floating islands of Lake Titicaca. These islands are made almost completely out of reeds that grow in the lake and support entire lifestyles on the islands themselves! These were another vision to be had only one place in the world!

Service

One short-term team was spending a day in a garbage dump. In Peru, there is a whole community of people who live in and around the garbage dump. These people dig through the refuse each day to seek out recyclables, organic material to be fed to animals, scrap wood or metal for building, and anything else that can be reutilized. On this day, the short-term team would enter into the dump to bring what joy they could through prayer, encouragement, and love for these brothers and sisters. We joined them.

It was a joy for those of us who were learning Spanish on our trip to be able to translate for others! For one of the first times in our race, we were the experienced veterans. This short-term team followed our lead in both words and action as we greeted each individual with a loving smile. We each took a small group of volunteers with us and went in different directions.

At first, the volunteers seemed awkward and clumsy with their words. They did not know what to say or how to act. But with each new person we met, they became more confident. At the beginning of the morning, I conducted the conversations with the natives and the short-termers simply watched with smiles. As the morning progressed, they began to pray in English after I was finished conversing and I would translate their prayers into Spanish for them. By the time we left, I barely was a part of the conversation. I simply translated their words into Spanish and joyfully watched them connect in a way that seemed so foreign to them when they had first arrived.

This was one of the most unexpected joys I had throughout the entire race. Being a hands-on person, I had always valued putting personal sweat and effort into a project. The joy that beamed from their faces as we waved goodbye and entered back into the vans will stay with me for years to come!

Life Lesson: It just as important to foster others' ability to share love as it is to share your own. It is also a joy to see others pour themselves into an altruistic endeavor and simply be able to help facilitate it.

When we selected a particular ministry to focus each of our individual efforts on, I selected IncaThaki. IncaThaki is a discipleship program for young boys. While spending time with Joca, who founded the project years ago and continues its operations to this day, I was able to gain a clearer perspective of the project's vision. Joca had started it because he had grown up on the streets of Trujillo. He had seen how the poverty in the city turns young men to crime, drugs, and self-destruction. He wanted to offer them something more. He began IncaThaki. IncaThaki offers sports ministry to young boys. Three days each week, the facility is open during the mornings and afternoons for the boys to simply come play floorball (hockey), volleyball, skateboard, or cards. Joca does a short devotional with the boys each day and then gives them more time to play. He personally invests in each of these boys on a daily basis and has for years!

This investment has paid off in dividends. Boys that he began working with three years ago when they were thirteen are now sixteen and mentoring the younger boys. Boys he began working with three years ago when they were ten are now thirteen and beginning to recognize what responsibility means. Boys under the age of ten have brought him other boys because they found them alone on the street with no one to care for them. They all care for one another now. They are family. ***This is what the Kingdom of Heaven is supposed to look like here on Earth.***

It was a privilege to be a part of this family for the few weeks I was in Trujillo.

IncaLink provided many services beyond that of hosting short-term mission teams. We were fortunate to experience the breadth of these while spending time in Peru. They included:
- *IncaThaki*
    - *sports ministry three times each week with daily devotionals*
    - *free neighborhood floorball ministry each Saturday in a nearby park*
    - *hiking and sandboarding treks with the boys from IncaThaki*
- *Elim*
    - *garbage dump ministry*
    - *weekly children's programs with Bible lessons, songs, and playing*
    - *weekly adult church programs with Bible studies*
- *Amijai*
    - *weekly neighborhood children's ministry*
    - *providing Bible lessons, games, songs, and fellowship to the poorest communities on the edge of the city*
- *Mana*
    - *provides day care for the children of the garbage dump workers*
    - *provides food for the children while their parents work*
    - *provides school supplies so the children can receive the full education available*
    - *provides games, crafts, and sports for the children to play*
- *Pasitos de Fe*
    - *maintains a home for children of Trujillo (orphanage)**

This was still getting started while we were there and they were only allowed to keep the two boys they had enrolled during the day. It was still a work in progress, but the two boys were provided daily care nevertheless. The boys were given care they did not receive anywhere else while basic building constructions continued.

Opening Doors

I'm sitting in the dark, staring at a brick wall.

I am in an enclosed room. There are four walls, but no door. The windows give me a glimpse of the world outside.

I cannot help but notice what a raw analogy this is to so many lives. We have fortified ourselves with explanations of faith. We have encircled our lives with feelings of understanding. We have guarded our viewpoints with sentiments of justice. But while building our protection, we forgot to create a door to let others in. And now we're isolated by our own hand with only windows to show us what some of the world beyond us can be.

***

A voice calls me to the place where a door would be. As I come closer, flaming sparks begin to pour in through holes in the wall.

We all have reasons to be afraid of the greater world beyond our walls.

Although the sparks present a danger undeniable, eventually they subside. The voice calls me to the same place. I am given instructions to discern three points on the walls that must be broken.

How often are we challenged to break free from our intentions? How many times have friends or family brought to our attention habits that limit our potential? How great could we be if only we would begin to listen?

So I pick up a hammer. I smash the top barrier. As the metal clangs to the floor it resembles stories and worldviews that did not come from me, but have been given to me throughout my life by others. This is my naiveté. The second piece takes a few hits, but doesn't budge. I move on to the bottom stronghold. It looks strong, but breaks off easily. This is my pride. Now that this is no longer intact, the second piece falls away with one strong swing. This is my fear.

Naiveté. Pride. Fear. If we could break these out of our lives, what a life we could know beyond our greatest imaginings, beyond the walls we have built up around us.

***

The wall opens. Where once there was only a barrier, now there is a door. I squint as I step through. My eyes take but a brief moment adjusting to what is before me. A world I never knew awaits.

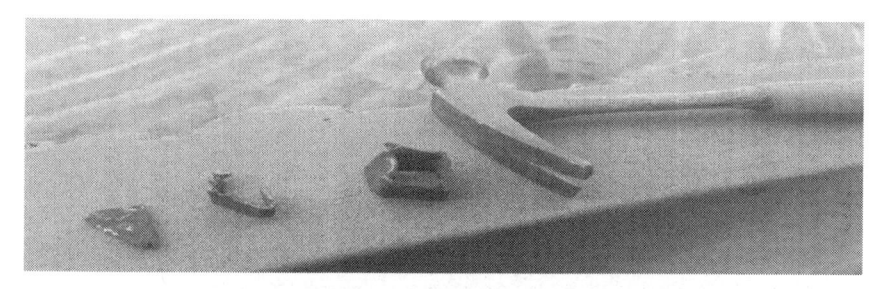

Unexpected Greeting

Joca asked our team for some help on our "off-day". I said yes. Ryan came with me to help Joca serve a children's program Sunday night. Walking back from the bus stop, as we rounded the corner with the soccer field, a small voice called out "*Patricio, Patricio!*" We turned to see a little boy waving at us from the other side of the field. He shouted "*Patricio!*" as he waved and "*Hola, Rafael!*" (Ryan went by Rafael.) After we waved back, he ran off towards a nearby house.

Favorite Moments in Peru

1. Singing *Turn the Page* with Missy at IncaLink talent show
2. Spending my "off-day" taking the IncaThaki boys and Brenda's girls to church
3. Spending the day with Pepe, Gato, and Elena at the mall before kids' night w Joca
4. Sandboarding after our team hike
5. Swing dancing with Claire
6. Visiting Machu Picchu and Los Uros

Bolivia

Summary

There is no comparison. The hardest month I had on the Race was in Bolivia.

We started our month in Bolivia with a twenty-hour bus ride, followed by a ten-hour train ride. This had followed a three-hour border crossing that had occurred after an eight-hour bus ride had already taken place. Needless to say, by the time we got to our destination, we were ready for some relaxation.

Upon our arrival, around 12:30 a.m., we were informed there was one bedroom for the girls inside the house. The boys would be sleeping in the partially constructed church extension outside. We sighed and set up our tents.

After settling in, the accommodations were actually not too hard. We had been forewarned to be ready to sleep with only what we had in our packs from the beginning of our training camp. This was simply the first time I actually needed to and it just seemed worse than it was at the time because we had to set it all up in the dark after an exhausting journey. The worst part about sleeping outside was the mosquitoes and the heat. For anyone who has been camping in a Texas summer, this is fairly standard.

We had a family that treated us like their own the whole time they hosted us! They prepared meals for us, chatted with us pleasantly, shared movie nights with their kids, and were gracious to have us there helping their little local church. They had never hosted a World Race or mission team before, so we were all learning together. The work they asked us to do was substantial, but relatively easy with enough persistence.

It was nothing on the field that made this month hard for me. It was what was happening at home. My brother had his third girl during March of this year. She had been expected to have complications after birth and was then born premature, which caused even more problems. She had been in the hospital ever since she was born. While in Bolivia, I received a phone call from our squad mentor. This had never happened before. She told me that my mom had called their emergency hotline and said I needed to get ahold of my brother immediately. I thanked her and quickly hung up, so I could call my brother. He told me his little girl had been diagnosed as terminal. She was given two to three weeks to live.

This was the first time I had heard my brother's voice since I had left nine months earlier.

I tried to extend my sympathies as best I could over the phone. Some words will just never carry the weight they're supposed to. As we said goodbye, I did not know how to feel. I was so far away from my brother and he had suffered so much. I had not been there.
I wish I could say I immediately decided to come home and support my family. But I didn't. I had never known Hannah. She had been born while I was on the race. Now it seemed she was going to die while I was on the race. It is hard to mourn a life you have never known. I shared with my team and host family the news I had received. They prayed for me. I thought about different ways I could support my brother. I could only send emails once each week. I could call everyday. He could call me. None of it seemed enough. The next day I decided I would go home. The airport was five hours away. The girls would be going into the city about a week after I got the call to do ministry there. I booked a flight to coincide with the day they were going into the city.

That was one of the longest weeks of my life.

Every day I feared I would get a phone call saying she had passed. I had been too late. No call ever came.
The girls actually changed their plans and headed into the city

a few days later than expected. Nevertheless I was going to catch my plane. Our host's sister made the drive and our host himself accompanied me for the five hours on the way. When I checked in, they told me my plane had been delayed by two hours. It was possible I would miss my connecting flight in Miami because this left less than an hour for me to make my connection, which would have to include going through international customs. I made it.

A week after I had received the call, I walked into the Dallas/Fort Worth airport. It felt different than I remembered. All the shops were closed. The airport was shut down. It must have been one of the last flights of the night. Twenty minutes after the plane landed, nobody was left. I looked around for my mom who was going to pick me up. She was nowhere to be found. I walked into a neighboring gate with no luck. As I returned down the escalator to the original gate, my mother waved up at me. She wiped the tears from her eyes as she embraced me. I was home.

***

I fell asleep at my mom's house that night. She left for work and I called my brother the following morning. He said he was going to the hospital after doing some work from home. I joined him at home and it felt good to be with him. We went up to the hospital after having lunch with my brother's wife. She had just left after spending all morning with their little girl.

I met Hannah for the first time that day.

She lay there while my brother and I leaned over her bed. Shortly after arriving, he had explained the gist of her journey to me. We continued to watch her sleep. Silence filled the room. He had mentioned that it was difficult because people don't know what to say or do when they come to support him. I joked that this must be one of those times. He said it certainly was. We began to talk about other things. We caught up on what strange experiences I had on the Race, how his other girls were, and what kinds of plans we still hoped for. He asserted there was not much they could hope for after the diagnosis. They were mainly hoping that they would be able to bring her home out of the hospital before she passes. We remained there in the room with Hannah all day.

Around eight or nine o'clock, we left to go back home. We stopped by one of our old restaurants we both enjoyed. I asked if he'd like to pray before the meal. He bowed his head. I prayed for the meal, but more than that I prayed that Hannah would live long enough so Randy could bring her home before God brings her home to Heaven. It was a hard prayer.

After we ate, I went back to my mom's to sleep. I returned to my brother's again the next morning. I arrived and he said, "We're going racing. I need to blow off some steam." This was a way to support my brother I had certainly not thought of, but was more than happy to accommodate! We drove to a go-kart racing track near my brother's house. It was great to just let loose a little for both of us!

The next few days blur together in my memory. I took an afternoon to have lunch with my previous business partner. She and I had become very close while working together as partners for four years. Another night my brother was working a concert at his church, so I had some time that would be free. I told a few friends I'd be at Starbucks for a few hours if they wanted to see me. I was happy to see some familiar faces. I have known many of my friends for the majority of my life, so it was a breath of fresh air to see them again! They had some new additions themselves.

Outside of these three or four hours, I spent all my time with my family. It was exactly what I had come home to do.

The last night I was there, I spent some time with my brother's wife and my mom in Hannah's room. My brother's wife, Angie, has one of the most optimistic outlooks on life I have ever encountered but, with all that was going on, what could she hope for. She hoped for the same thing that my brother did. She hoped to bring her daughter home and let her be part of the family. As I prepared to leave, I felt I needed to pray with her. My mom, my sister-in-law, and I joined hands around Hannah's bedside. I thanked God for the life He breathed into Hannah and asked Him to continue breathing it into her long enough for her to come home to Angie before going home to Jesus in Heaven.

I had booked a return flight to Bolivia on Sunday. We went to church together while Randy operated the media for the service. We went out to lunch afterwards and then said our goodbyes. As I hugged my brother, I told him I was proud of him. He chuckled with a tear. It was no joke. I am still so proud of him and his family. Over many years of working as a counselor, I have seen many ways that people suffer. Randy's family shares faith, hope, and love with one another as they suffer. These are the things that remain long after the suffering ceases. The faith, hope, and love they share with each other are an inspiration for these graces in more lives than they will ever know.

People asked me if going home was hard. It wasn't. Taking steps onto the plane heading to Bolivia, expecting that I would never see my niece again, were some of the heaviest footsteps I've ever had to make. But I knew that, as much as it meant for me to come home, my brother would have wanted me to continue my journey.

So it continued.

Service

Our ministry this month was with the local church that was operated solely by our host family. We helped teach children's Bible lessons, sang songs with the children, and played games with them. We participated in weekly volleyball nights with the church's youth. We joined our hosts during adult Bible studies they led. Primarily though, our work became physical labor. The church was nearly one hundred years old and sorely needed some upkeep. We were asked to repaint the walls in the Sunday School rooms, but this quickly turned into molding and plastering, patchwork, mold repair, and stucco work. This project became the bulk of the work we would do in Bolivia.

Admittedly, with my week away and some of the other projects that the rest of team worked on, which drew them away from the church location itself, some of our team felt that we had not done enough for this family who had treated us so well. They assured us that the labor we had done saved them thousands of dollars and they were very happy with our help. So much so that the last day we were there, they told us not to do any work even though we had planned to. They wanted to take us out for a picnic and swim in a nearby river. We left them the next morning with smiles.

Some of our extended family certainly resides in Roboré, Bolivia!

I Am Going Home

This is not my adventure.

I am going home.

In Bolivia, we have found a family that treats us like one of their own. We eat with them each meal. We greet their children as they come home from school. We enjoy movies together in the living room, counting down participants as each person slowly fades off to sleep.

When asked to provide games, lessons, or songs for the children, it is a joy to share with the little ones. When asked to help renovate the church building or share our testimonies with the congregation, it is a blessing to pour into the body of believers here in Robore. When asked to join the weekly volleyball games with the youth, it is as though we are playing with friends we have known for years. Though the country seems desolate, love is flourishing here.

I am grateful for these blessings, but they will not keep me here.

***

This journey has not been free of difficulties. Each country presents challenges adapting to local cultures. At each ministry we struggle to find balance between being overworked or underutilized. Everyday there are reminders of family and friends we are missing at home.

Clearing out the cobwebs in the outdoor shower each day allows ice-cold water to wash us clean. The sleeping pad on the bottom of a tent provides minimal relief from the concrete foundation underneath. Each country presents the hope of novel experiences, however the 20-30 hour bus rides each way do little to excite this in us.

I am grateful for these challenges; these will not be the reason I go home.

***

Having three men travel with a group of twenty women presents its own challenges. Graciously, a trip designed as an escape for us has been added to our itinerary. A 12-hour journey into uninhabited forest to spend days sharing grace and peace with an isolated military outpost. A calling into the wild that promises adventure unlike any other.

I am grateful for this opportunity…

…but this is not the option I will pursue.

I truly pray the other two men on my squad make the most of this gift. I pray that the men in the outpost receive joy and compassion through their presence. I pray that this journey offers both challenges and blessings to them both. And while I long to be with them as they overcome obstacles out in the unknown, I know this is not for me. This is their time. This is their adventure.

This is not my adventure.

I am going home.

More Than Pity

Walking through the Dallas/Fort Worth airport, it feels as though I am walking through a memory. Riding through the familiar streets of the suburb I've called home my whole life, it feels like being pulled through a dream. As I walk up to the door, a face I know very well greets me. She embraces me with tears streaming down her face, but her smile tells me these are tears of joy. I know that this is my mother.

***

A new day dawns. I meet a man who is working from home. This is a blessing to him because he has spent six hard months balancing work, caring for his two older girls, and daily visits to the hospital where his littlest warrior, Hannah, has spent her whole life. I am grateful to join him and his wife for lunch.

We spend the next six hours by Hannah's bedside. We talk of many things. Conversations range from daily frustrations to surprising joys and through a lifetime of memories shared; we find connections in the year we have been apart. I see so much love in his eyes when he looks at his daughter. I know that this is my brother.

***

I spend the limited days I have in the United States with this family and I see a strength in them that is admirable anywhere in the world. Every day is a life and death struggle for their newest child. But through the grace of their spirit, they take care to still spend family time together, never allowing their elder two girls to feel sidelined. They are honest with every struggle. Their daughters are learning valuable lessons of facing hardship with simplicity and responsibility.

These are hard lessons. I spend my last day there with my sister-in-law, Angie, and my mother in Hannah's room. Throughout the day, I learn my own lessons. I see Angie know just when to reposition her daughter. I see her know just how she likes to sit. I see the ways that care and compassion manifests itself in every situation. Even the situations that many would say have little hope can be made brighter by the presence of love that seeks to bring comfort, no matter the size or scope.

I see Angie carry this love through her pain. I see that her daughter has a happier day because of its presence. I see the love grow each time she smiles at her other daughters despite this incredible time of grieving. I know that the love Angie has for her daughter will last far longer than her daughter's life and that the memories will be hard. But I know that she will carry the love always. I know that this is my sister.

***

I am grateful for the wellspring of support this family has. I am grateful for the friends that have rallied beside them. I am grateful for the church body that provides relief in every way it can.

Above all, I am grateful I could return home to be with them because in my time at home, I saw their need. Money can help with the financial crisis that comes with a hospitalized child. Dinners can lighten the workload and volunteers can help balance occupational stress with focusing time on family. But these do not provide relief from suffering.

No amount of sympathy or pity or condolences can provide relief. Presence, instead, suffers with love. Sometimes the load cannot be lightened, but it can be shared.

***

My family has taught me so much throughout my life. This lesson is probably one of the most significant I have ever learned. If we say we will share love with the world, we must offer them more than pity. We must be willing to be present, both through trials and through tribulations.

Many people have asked me why I went home. I went home to be with my family as they suffer. Now many people ask me why I return to the field. I return to the field for the same reason: because somewhere in the world my brother is suffering. And so I go.

I go so my presence may remind him he does not suffer alone.

Unexpected Greeting

Shortly after walking into El Molino, a restaurant owned by our contact's siblings, which we frequented weekly, a little girl came up and hugged Dani. She then turned to put her arms around my neck and said, "*Hola, Patricio.*" I said "*hola*" as she smiled and turned to walk away. I turned to Missy and said, "Who was that?"

Missy said she didn't know either. Dani then explained that it was the girl we had swam with in the river the second day we had arrived in Bolivia. She is the cousin of our contact's children. This was three weeks after I had seen her the one and only previous time.

Favorite Moments in Bolivia

1. Aguas Caliente [Hot Springs] with the team, Klovis, Lisette, their children, Philipe, and his sons
2. Driving the dirt bike from church to El Molino with Gabriel
3. Sharing my experience of re-entering the race and inviting my squad to come with me on the 2-month journey at 2nd LDW (Leadership Development Workshop)

After returning to the field, I felt it was important to share the newfound appreciation I had for simply being present as a form of ministry. Additionally, I had discovered a new perspective in viewing the remainder of the Race as a two-month mission trip. It dawned on me that, if we had not already committed to an eleven-month mission, two months would seem like quite a significant commitment and opportunity!

I struggled with the urge to share this with the Squad, wondering if it was only my own vanity seeking some kind of self-serving importance. I prayed to God to create space for me to share and make it clear if He desired me to do so. The next day, the whole squad was gathered to listen to a sermon that would never come due to technical problems.

As my gaze circled the room I saw the entire squad waiting for a message and I saw our squad leaders debating on what to do. I stood up and asked Karissa if I could share a few words. She graciously allowed me the floor.

It was a pleasure to share with the Squad a new understanding that our mission is not always meant to change a person's life, but rather sometimes to simply be a part of it. It was a joy to invite them to apply this understanding to the opportunity we still had that many in this world will never know. It was refreshing to walk them through memories of why they had come on the Race to begin with.

I was grateful just to be walking this path with them anew.

Chile

Summary

This was the second month in a row that we would live and serve together with a family that adopted us as its own. In Chile, we worked with a mission church that serves the local community in Los Andes.

We arrived late in the evening after our travel day came to a conclusion. In true Latin American fashion, we were welcomed graciously! Our host family recognized that we must be tired and encouraged us to relax in our rooms. The girls found their rooms down the street in the home of a lay member of the church. The men slept in the Sunday School room next to the sanctuary. We unpacked our bags and began to settle in.

Then we heard lots of shuffling going on in the sanctuary. A couple of us went out to socialize with our new companions. It turned out they weren't just socializing. The pastor of the church we were working with was trying to move a projector. "Easy fix," we thought.

We volunteered to help out. After all, it's what we were there for. After we got the screws disconnected from the projector, we asked where he wanted to put it.

"I want to hang it from the ceiling," he told us [in Spanish].

Okay. So, this will be a little bit more of a project than we thought. Still not a problem to get it done before heading for bed. I climbed up onto the third tier of the scaffolding that's in the sanctuary and asked just where he would like me to hang it.

"Well, we'll have to put some holes in the ceiling to hang it from," he told me. This project was getting a little bit more cumbersome than expected. Once I was able to hold it in position near the ceiling, it was evident that it would not be able to reach the screen.

"We'll just have to move the screen into the center of the stage and switch places with the cross that's on the wall."

At that point, we all decided this was a project that could wait until morning. The next day was pretty full of activities, so we didn't get back to this until the evening. And then again the next as well. What started as a project that was simply moving a projector became a project of creating holes to mount the base, then connecting the projector to the base, then splicing electrical wires to line the wall from the floor to the ceiling (since there is no outlets anywhere near the ceiling), then switching a screen and cross, mounting both of these in their new positions and then lining the wall with a connecting cable from the projector to an expected laptop.

The first three days in Chile turned to three late nights quickly.

***

Our host family treated us warmly and welcomed us graciously into their home! It was a mission church that had a small enough operation to allow the husband and wife to run the church fully without support from any staff.

We soon found out why it was so easy to do so. The church has a congregation of only 4-10 people, aside from the pastor and his wife.

It was apparent what one of the priorities would be for us: inviting members of the community to come join the small congregation. We first did this through a youth invitational project. Our host took us to local schools and visited classrooms inviting young people to a new Saturday evening program the church would be starting while we were with them. We also passed out flyers in the streets to youth, in order to advertise the project. Our pastor said that together we had passed out a total of about 1,000 flyers. He was hoping that we would be able to bring in 10 participants.

On the first Saturday, 10 youth came walking in the church's doors for the first time. We continued to invite youth throughout the month to each Saturday; unfortunately the novelty must have worn off. The number of participants trickled down to 3 or 4 each week. Still, this is a significant increase for a congregation that only has 10 members to begin with!

***

During our time in Chile, we witnessed the most authentic example of a unified church many of us had ever seen.

Los Andes is the border town of Chile to Argentina's Mendoza. They are separated by only a few hours' drive through a highway pass in the Andes Mountains. Occasionally, this pass receives too much snow to allow vehicles through to the other side. It was one of these occasions that brought two church families together.

For about a week and a half to two weeks, our host had a guest family staying with him. It wasn't until the third day that we discovered he had not known this family until they came knocking on his door! The guest family was a pastor, his wife, and his children from Mendoza, who were coming home from a vacation in Chile. The pass was closed due to being snowed in and the guest family stopped at our host's church to ask for refuge.

By the way they were interacting with one another, we had thought they had been old friends! The guest family stopped in only because they needed refuge and they saw that the church was a Baptist church, just as theirs is in Mendoza. Our host then simply accepted them as family immediately, providing them with food, lodging, and fellowship for as long as they needed.

Simple. Unquestioning. True compassion.

We would go on to stay with this guest family the following month, as we were looking for future contacts to work with. They welcomed us into their home and will certainly be a wonderful host for any future teams to visit.

They never would have been on our radar if the snow hadn't kept them in Chile longer than expected. They had need and sought help from their church family. Though they were unknown before, their brotherhood was immediately honored and provided for.

We should all be ready to care for one another in such a manner.

Service

    Our service opportunities centered primarily with refurbishing aspects of the church building and inviting members to participate in its services. Every Sunday, as the grown-ups were participating in the adult church service, a couple of us would lead a children's Sunday School. This was done with the help of a guided Bible lesson manual the children followed each week. We would play games with them, lead them through the Bible lesson, help them to memorize a key Bible verse, and then help walk them through sharing it with their parents at the end of the adult service.

    The church had clothing for sale during a weekly street market as well. One cold week, our team leader came up with the idea of giving out coffee and cookies to pedestrians passing by. This greatly increased the number of pedestrians who stopped to rummage through the clothes for sale!

    We also helped sand down the stage in the sanctuary to repaint it. A couple of us built a concrete foundation for a new shower being put in for incoming short-term teams. We then proceeded to build the shower itself and connect the pipes together. It worked! A shower had never felt so satisfying as it did when I took it in a shower that I built with help from a few companions and my own two hands!

    Inviting participants to church in a variety of ways continued to be a focus of our ministry throughout the entire month. My favorite experience with this was also the last ministry opportunity I would have. Our host had sought out a number of evangelistic skits and stunts online. We put together two of them that he thought would be a good outreach during the weekly street market.
    One of these was a series of us representing separate vices and being concerned with only ourselves. Each of our own vices

led us to self-destruction. Throughout the entire skit, we only spoke saying "yo" which means "I" or "me" in Spanish. A teammate representing the Christian gospel then showed us that it wasn't about us. It was about God. After our teammate introduced us to the gospel message, we began saying "Él" meaning "Him." This freed us to work together and overcome our vices.

The second skit began with two clowns. We were competing with one another to market a table that said we could fix anything. We resolved to work together. A little child walked by with a balloon and it got popped. We put it back together poorly and handed it back to her. We were very satisfied with ourselves. A man and woman entered the picture next. They were in love. Then another woman came on the scene. The man left the first woman for the second and the original woman fell dead with a broken heart. We picked her up and put her on our table; confidently knowing we would be able to fix her. We were unable to put her back together and each had torn her heart to pieces even more. We walked off in separate directions and hoped nobody would know we were unable to help her! As she lay there, another teammate came up with a Bible in hand. She opened up the Bible and pulled out a brand new heart. She put it on the body lying on the table and the original woman came back to life. Our original sign was torn off the background banner to reveal "Only Jesus Saves" [in Spanish].

After these two skits had been performed, we walked through the crowd that had gathered to watch them, inviting them to attend the church. We were only about a block away from the actual building.

Later in the evening, we would go to the main square of the city to perform our final outreach. This would become a phenomenal opportunity to draw interest in a way none of us could ever have expected! I was dressed up in a white robe with a purple sash draped around me. Then a crown of thorns was placed on my head. A cross was handed to me. The cross was too big to fit in the car. I would be carrying it to the center of town... sixteen blocks *away.*

Needless to say, we drew a few viewers along the way! One person actually stopped to ask if we needed a ride to where we were going. Once we arrived at the center square, my six teammates walked out into the crosswalk while the light was red. They held up signs in their hands saying "Jesus Te Ama" (Jesus Loves You). I began to struggle across the street with the cross on my back. Their signs turned around to reveal the words "Fue Por Ti" (It Was For You). I leaned up against the post wantonly and waited for the light to change, all the while with the cross burdening my shoulders.

We had planned to do this only for about twenty minutes, and then repeat the other two skits in the square. The street crossing stunt must have drawn more interest than our host expected, because he opted to continue repeating this process for an hour and a half. Every eye in the square and every driver's glance was focused on this Jesus crossing the street, carrying a real cross while struggling to carry the burden it caused!

One of the sweetest experiences I had on the entire Race took place during this exercise. Many times during this skit, parents would walk by and ask their children to identify who I was. The children would answer "Jesus" with a newfound confidence in everything they'd heard about the man who carried His cross for the sins of us all! One child in particular wouldn't be satisfied with passively knowing who he was looking at.

I crossed the street with the usual struggle, falling to my knees along the way. I pulled myself up on the light post on the curb. I leaned my head back against the cross, which was between the post and me. I felt a little tug at my robe, down by my knees. I lowered my glance to see a hesitant little face looking up at me. He held in his hand a half-eaten churro. With trembling nervous eyes, he lifted his churro up to my hand. My heart dropped out from under me!

As I took the churro from his hand, he quickly turned around and darted back to his mother who was a few feet away. I smiled at him and the crowd that had watched him offer his help to me. "*Él es mi hijo (He is my son),*" I proclaimed. His mother and I exchanged a smile as he nuzzled himself into her side. They walked away together.

That child has the heart and soul that we all strive for. It is not enough to see suffering and to recognize it. We are called to help those we can. On that day, the message came in the form of a little boy who looked more like Christ than I did.

Unexpected Greeting

"*Hola, Ryan! Hola, Jesus!*" came a voice from behind us. As we turned, we saw the faces of a group of teenagers we had talked to in the park about ten days ago. Originally, we had approached them to invite them to come to a weekly youth program the church was hosting. We ended up speaking to them for about 90 minutes, covering topics ranging from school woes to travel desires.

They now approached us as we had been doing a street evangelism effort that had five people holding signs spelling *"Jesus Te Ama"* (Jesus Loves You) on one side and *"Fue Por Ti"* (It Was For You) on the other. Then I walked across the street dressed as Jesus carrying the cross. These teenagers had recognized us and come over to say hello.

PATRICK BOOTH

Favorite Moments in Chile

1. Touring Viña San Esteban with Missy
2. "Jesus crossing" in Los Andes
   --the little boy handing me a churro
3. Visiting Easter Island with Charis and Karissa
4. Hiking uncharted with Dani, Luyen and Barrett

Argentina

Summary & Service

Our final month on the field together.

This month was a different experience than all the rest. Coming into this month, we were tired.

We were tired of our teammates.

We were tired of ministry.

We were tired of "living in community."

We were just tired of the Race itself.

The novelty of the Race had worn off and we were left with simply uncomfortable conditions. My team also would be doing Unsung Heroes for the first time. This meant our primary mission would be to find new host organizations for Adventures in Missions to work with in the future.

However, they had already put together a couple of contacts that they wanted us to scout for them. A typical Unsung Heroes month would consist of meeting new people and introducing the Race to them. Ours would be more about visiting people who are already familiar with Adventures in Missions and checking to see that future teams would be okay visiting them. There was a feeling that we would be visiting people the home organization had already approved, simply for them to be able to say they had somebody check it out in person.

Right from the beginning, it felt like we would be doing nothing.

Our final journey began with three of our four teams traveling together to San Rafael, Argentina. In San Rafael, two of our teams would continue their ministry helping the Christian hostel for the full month. Our team would be leaving about a week after we arrived, to head towards Mendoza.

Before we left we would have an opportunity to simply relax

together, which was greatly needed at this point in our travels. Siesta hours were consistent day to day. Everyday from 1:30-4:30 p.m., everything in the town was closed. There was little activity going on during the days with any of us. This suited us just fine.

Some nights we shared meals with our hosts and others we would be on our own. Our hosts had been a missionary family working independently of any direct church affiliation for nearly thirty years! They had raised their children on the mission field, served together throughout their entire journey, and shared with us many insights from their formidable experience!

Before our team would depart from their company, we would have a few opportunities to help prime the hostel for continued service. These included:
- *draining the remaining water in the pool that the pump could not get to*
- *this was done by hand with pitchers and buckets*
- *helping begin to clear the field of fall foliage*

Our second ministry experience took us back to the border town of Mendoza. This is where we would have the opportunity to follow up with the guest family we met in Chile. They were wonderful hosts!

Just as the families in Bolivia and Chile, this family welcomed us into their home as though they had known us our whole lives. Although the men again stayed in the church and the women on the teams stayed in the house, we spent the entire time we had in Mendoza together.

We only had three days there, but it certainly left a strong impression on us! Our host family took us out around the town to show us a historic site, local parks, and beautiful scenic overlooks of the city as a whole. They provided delicious meat for us, which was cooked right out back over an open flame on top of a table!

We were very grateful to be able to further the relationship with this family, especially because it was an unplanned part of our journey that seemed to have too many coincidences not to be ordained by the Holy Spirit!

This family truly treated us as their own. They did not ask us to serve in many ways during the three days we were there, except to participate in their children's program on Saturday morning and then to put together the service for their Sunday morning worship program. I am proud to say that our team took fifteen minutes of planning and was ready to do it!

(This is the other side of the novelty wearing off. Yes, it is disheartening to realize that worship is not always spontaneous and pure, but after you have been called to perform it so many times it becomes rather easy to put together.)

The worship that Sunday went off without a hitch. We all had become comfortable with various roles throughout a service and smoothly transitioned from one to another. This was a good morning for our team and for the family we served.

Our experiences in Mendoza allowed a little healing within our team's morale. It had been a good weekend and we were ready to move on together to our final ministry destination. This would be Buenos Aires.

A few members of our team were very much looking forward to spending our remaining ministry time in such a diversified modern city. There was considerable disappointment when we arrived at our destination: the Buenos Aires region, not the city.

There were no modern amenities. We were not even in a surrounding city of Buenos Aires. We were in a field. A field with houses. These houses were put together by the hands that lived there and with the materials they were able to collect. They were drafty enough that the bugs would come and go as they pleased. The cold or heat moved just as freely within the houses as the bugs. There was no Internet or phones. The electricity was shoddy. Our shower ran ice cold directly from the pipes underground. The toilet was used with discretion because every time you flushed a little leaked out onto the floor. It was not bolted securely into the ground. Food was minimal. Most meals were pasta. No sauce or seasoning or side dishes, just pasta. Water was tapped from a pipe outside the kitchen into the pitchers to serve.

This was the experience I had been expecting since signing up for the World Race. Now, after ten previous months of various living conditions, it was more frustrating than I imagined.

There was certainly no shortage of work to be done. Its tenants ran this community. This was one of five communities throughout Argentina that truly embody the idea of the early church.

All things are shared.
All members take care of one another.
There is no fee, no rent, no membership or restrictions for inclusion.
These communities serve those who need them.
Period.

These *granjas* form communities throughout Argentina that provide living quarters, food, and love to all who come to call the place home. This one seemed to include primarily young adults and children; it is not an orphanage, but something more. It is a community that a person can grow up into and when they do, they can continue the legacy by providing for others.

This is what we had signed up for.

Our two weeks at this final ministry allowed us a breadth of opportunities, both practical and experiential. We were each asked to share a bit of our background with the people living there and some of the things we had learned on the Race.

I felt grateful for this opportunity and spoke that first night. Our host was patient with us throughout the remaining two weeks, but diligently reminded us of his request. Each of us shared our histories and experiences. I believe this was truly an opportunity to encourage others' faith because many of the tenants living in the community were little more than a few years younger than our team!

We also were given an opportunity to speak at the combined church gathering that occurs each week from all of the communities within reasonable distance. They thanked us for our service and encouraged us on our way.

The ladies' ministry on our team took place 24/7 while living in the "granja." They each lived in separate houses with the people we were serving. They gave of themselves unceasingly during those two weeks.

We were able to help prepare meals, play with the children, and walk them to school. We dug out holes for pillars, positioned rebar, and demolished rotten walls. We were guests at two quinceñeras, led children's Bible lessons, and spent one morning visiting a prison.

Nine to twelve hour workdays were not uncommon. While this could be exhausting, it was also a great gift to know (not believe or think or wonder) that we were of service to the community.

After such an extensive experience in the field, one begins to see that short-term missions have their limitations. By this time I had learned that offering encouragement, hope, and appreciation to the full-time missionaries serving in each ministry we visit is just as important, if not more important, than our direct service. Two opportunities would stand out in this way.

***

One week before we finish our time in Buenos Aires our host had tells me that he visits a prison routinely. He describes an incredible story about one of their staff being falsely accused of abusing a member of the community. This staff member has since been sitting in jail for nine months without facing his trial. Each time our host visits, he notices that there are inmates who serve the others during their visitation time. He asks if this is some kind of *work duty. To his surprise, he is told that these men are the inmates that do not have visitors come see them! They volunteer their time as a way to interact with anyone other than their guards or fellow inmates.*

Our host asks if he can visit them. After that he returns many times and simply meets someone new each time! Astonished, I tell him there is no way that this could happen in the States because a person must be on an inmate's list, in order to visit them. To my surprise, he tells me it is the same there in Argentina! He has simply told his friend to tell the inmates that do not have visitors to put him on their lists. He then comes to visit them as they wait to meet someone new in their visitation that they have never known before!

I am astounded by the fervor of this man's love! He has taken his own time, as well as time that he could be visiting with his own friend, to meet and talk to inmates that he does not know in any way. All simply so that they may feel less alone than they are!

He goes on to tell me that this has created quite a community within the prison now. There is a faith community within the prison that encourages one another, cares for one another, and supports one another. This faith community exists solely because of a false accusation and two men's desire to share love in unimaginable ways!

This is an incredible opportunity that seems clearly evident to have the workings of the Holy Spirit at hand! I ask if I can visit the prison as well. He excitedly tells me that he would love to have me join him. Justin and I wake up around 5:30 in the morning, so that we can ride out with him when he goes. We arrive at the prison after picking up the man's father and family along the way. It is a long walk from the parking lot to the visitation area at the back of the prison grounds.

We drop off goods for the inmate before entering the line to check into visitation. (In Argentina, it is necessary for families to provide for inmates. Inmates are not provided personal toiletries or even food on the weekends.) After waiting in line for an hour or so, we are informed by the guard at the check-in desk that Justin and I will not be allowed in. Justin quickly tells our host that we will be happy to wait while they visit. Our host suggests trying the line again after most of the people have cleared out of it. He says sometimes rules can change a little when there is no one paying attention.

We wait on the concrete floor for another hour. We make use of our ample time to talk, sharing many experiences prior to the race that normally would never have come up with one another. As the line dies, we try the attendant again. He reinforces that, since we do not have passports with us, we will not be allowed to visit this day.

With that, we return to the car. Our conversations continue for another couple hours before our host returns to take us home. He returns alone and says that he has come out early since he knew we were waiting. The family will still be visiting for the better part of the day.

A part of our conversations have been that we would like to show our host that we appreciate him. We offer to treat him to lunch on the way back to the "granja." He accepts.

There is no glorious conversation. There is nothing particularly special about the restaurant. The meal is good, but not exceptional. **The commonality is what makes this meal special.** We eat, talk, and share each other's company as though we are old friends. This experience is one of my favorite opportunities to let someone know that their spirit is ours and our spirit is theirs.

Sometimes the greatest ministry you can provide is simply to let someone know they are not alone.

***

My final opportunity to reach out beyond the missionary/recipient relationship would be on our last day, during our last ride from our host:

Our host has gladly volunteered to drive us into the actual city of Buenos Aires, where we will meet the other two teams before making our final trek to our final debrief. Along the way, he asks if we are in a rush or if we have time to lunch with the neighboring community along the route. A teammate honestly says we do not have any agenda in Buenos Aires, so our drive is extended a number of hours. (You see, in Latin America, it is not uncommon that when you are invited to have lunch with someone, you are actually invited to join them for conversation before, during, and after the meal.)

We are all ready to be done with ministry by this time. It is not that we do not enjoy it or that it is particularly demanding. The best way to describe it may be like being at a family reunion. Everybody knows each other and is friendly to one another. There is no need for impressing anyone. Nevertheless, there is always a mild sense of watching what you say or how you act. This little pressure can be exhausting after eleven months.

Our team knows this is the last day of contact with official ministry partners, so we wait patiently and converse cordially. We are joined briefly by the founder of the program and take the time to express our thanks for the amazing communities he has put together. Then our journey continues onward towards Buenos Aires.

Shortly thereafter, in the middle of the road without warning, the vehicle sputters to a stop. After a few tries with the key, our host guesses that it has run out of gas. He explains that the gas gauge does not work and that it must not have been filled enough. He says he will have to find a gas station.

I immediately volunteer to go with him.

The gas station ends up being a little longer hike than I expect. We retrace the road about six to eight blocks. Along the way, we pick empty soda and water bottles from the trash to use as receptacles for the gasoline. Our host and I guess how much gas we will need to reach Buenos Aires and for him to return back to the "granja." With three 3-liter bottles in his hand and two 3-liters along with a 6-liter bottle in my own, we arrive at the gas station.

The attendant tells us that we can only fill up the 6-liter bottle. The others cannot be used. (I guess it is because the 3-liter bottles are all soda bottles and the 6-liter bottle is a water bottle.) Our host purchases three plastic gas cans from the station, we fill them up, and begin to make our way back to the vehicle.

The way back to the vehicle seems much shorter than the journey from it. (Journeys often feel this way: the way back almost always seems shorter and/or easier.) But more than that, our conversation seems to maintain a casual air. I share two stories about when I ran out of gas myself in the past. We begin to talk about cars in general and this proves to be a natural conversation for both of us that keeps our minds free from stress. The two of us could be any two people sharing a typical day's walk to and from an everyday chore.

We pour the gas into the chamber right there in the street.

He climbs back into the driver's side as I walk the plastic gas cans to a nearby trash bin. We climb back into the vehicle and are immediately aware of the tension in the air. I can see clearly that my team has been far more stressed out about this experience than I have been. In this experience I learn one final lesson.

Life Lesson: Difficult situations in ministry are often handled best by simply putting yourself into the position of the person you are serving and immersing yourself fully in the problem.

Solutions, peace, hope, faith, and love, are all found readily when you work through problems with others, rather than for them.

I was grateful for this final lesson and, honestly, for the opportunity I had to spend more one on one time with our host. I enjoyed his company throughout the entire month. That continued on our final walk to and from the gas station.

All of us passed most of the remaining ride quietly. We pulled up to our hostel where we would stay the last night before our final debrief. Our host asked us to unload quickly because he was letting

THE LONG ROAD HOME

us out on an active city street. We unpacked the vehicle, made short goodbyes, and began moving our bags inside.

I turned as my team moved into the hostel lobby. I opened the passenger door to the vehicle and reached my hand across the seat. Our host reached out his hand and shook mine briefly.

"Thank you for allowing us to be a part of your ministry this month. Your community truly embodies the Kingdom of Heaven here in Argentina. I believe many teams will be lucky to serve here in the future," I declared in my best Spanish.

"Gracias, hermano," he replied.

We shared a smile and a final clench.
We let go of each other's hands.
And we went our separate ways.

This is Not the End

"It's just too late to start living like family now."
"Whatever, guys, three more weeks."
"Our team is all sick of each other, but we're all just waiting it out now."

These are the statements I've heard all around me since we started our journey to our final country. The World Race is no longer the exciting journey it was when it started. The novelty has worn away to routine doldrums. The promise of living in community has become a cacophony of incessant social stimulation. In truth, most participants remain solely because they are resolved to finish what they started. With the finish line in sight, everyone keeps plodding along.
This is no way to end.
How can we take a year full of joys and turn it into regret? How can animosity abound in a community grounded in love? How can we share a Kingdom of Heaven when we are unwilling to invest the grace and love required to maintain that Kingdom, even amongst ourselves?
We cannot.
Eleven months is enough time for everyone to discover something an alumni told me I would come crashing into. "Everyone on the race hits a wall where they just wanna be at home." For some it's in month one, others month three or four. There's a phrase passed around about "The month seven desert". Lucky racers won't hit it till month nine or ten. Here, at month eleven, it's hard to find somebody that hasn't hit this wall.
Now, with three weeks of ministry left, it is time to reevaluate our original intentions, but this time, they must be evaluated with ten months of experience weighing the decision. Here, in the final leg of our journey, we must ask ourselves if we would do it all over again. Now, as we prepare for the next chapter in our life, we

must consider what will be taken from this journey and into the next.

For some, it is an important realization that the mission field is not where they are called to serve. For others, new callings have been revealed to engage their communities at home. I do not know where my next journey will take me. But I know I am unwilling to take bitterness, resentment, animosity, and regret there with me.
It is time for a choice.
My bitterness will turn to joy. My resentment gradually subsides to gratitude. My animosity slowly softens to compassion. My regrets form a foundation of new understandings.
This is not the end.
This is the beginning.

Unexpected Greeting

We exit the final worship service of our newfound community. It is heavily crowded. Missy, Claire and I find a place to discreetly wait with a few of the youth from our *granja*. As we are waiting, two young men turn away from their conversation to greet me.
"*Hola, Patricio,*" they begin. "*Como estas?*"
"*Bien, gracias,*" I reply. "*Y tu?*"
"*Bien, bien,*" they assert.
They return then to their original conversation next to us.
I ask Missy who the two men were. She reminds me that these are two of the men who live in our *granja*. We don't work with them because we spend most of our time with the children, but they are aware of our presence and express their gratitude with familiarity.

Three Beds

Our final ministry in Argentina was with Adulam, a wonderfully example of God's Kingdom at work. Adulam makes up five different communities throughout Argentina that provide food, shelter and fellowship to those who need respite. The one that we worked with for two weeks served primarily orphans and young families.

For most of the second week, Justin, Ryan and I had been part of a reconstruction project. We spent the first few days demolishing rotted walls, the middle of the week constructing pillars, and the last few days digging holes to place the pillars. We asked what the building would be used for.

"A home," Marcos answered.

Marcos, our host for the two weeks there and director of this Adulam location, went on to explain that the community had reached its full capacity. He illustrated that he received nearly weekly calls from new families needing aid, despite the fact that there were no more beds.

He asked us to pray to God for direction and guidance because his heart felt a great need to help the last family that had called, but there were three members and he had no place to put them. He did not want to turn them away.

We prayed together.

As we were saying our goodbyes a few days later, one of the young boys we worked with joyfully asked if we had heard the news. He was clearly very excited about something we had no knowledge of. We asked what had happened. He told us that a generous couple from one of the other Adulam communities had adopted him and his two sisters!

We congratulated him for the adoption and that all of his siblings had been adopted together. We later asked Marcos if he had heard. He smiled.

"Sometimes God speaks very clearly."

The Long Road Home

The race is finished.
The journey has ended.
All the tears have been shed.
All the laughter has been shared.
Looking back, the misfortunes we experienced seem diminished. The struggles feel lighter. The arguments lose relevance and resentments are released. As we reminisce, memorable joys bring smiles to our faces. Inexplicable peace fills us with gladness. Compassion is strengthened and love will be held ready for when we meet again.

What is the change that takes place within us? How can our perceptions be transformed so greatly? Why does the impossible seem probable?

The Spirit within us grows.

We have a strength we have never known and burdens that used to weigh us down feel light. Within us is a grace that we did not believe exists and attacks that used to spur our rage now irritate us no more than an uncomfortable breeze. Wisdom has found us and confusion that used to ensnare our efforts is untangled as simply as a child's puzzle.

With the Spirit, we see before us a path we have never known. A path that sparks an ominous sensation, but feels familiar like we have been here in a dream. This path is riddled with cracks and crevices that easily ensnare but, with understanding of its patterns, forward progression is easily manifested.

This path is the same path I have walked my entire life. It has not changed, nor will it. Yet today it bares no threat. It is no different. I am different.

I am finally ready for the long road home.

Favorite Moments in Argentina

1. Missy's prayer circle team time in San Rafael
2. Visiting the prison and lunch with Marcos and Justin
3. "Adventure day" exchanging money with Dani

Epilogue
Crazy Healing

My first team could have been known as the allergy team. We had the most food allergies of any team. Three people were lactose intolerant, one teammate described his allergies being from "anything outdoors", and another with endometriosis added to more routine ailments.

Leah had been dealing with severe pain since 2005. She was put on hydrocodone three years prior to the Race. When it didn't help the pain after training camp in 2014 her doctor decided she had endometriosis, though in all likelihood she had it for quite some time before that. That's when the severe diet commenced. Additionally, she had been dealing with worsening allergies since 2009 or 2010: milk, nuts, etc.

When it came to allergies, she had stomach pain anywhere within a minute to an hour of eating something bad. It depended on what the food was what kind of stomach pain and when it would start: gas, bloating, and diarrhea. The endometriosis added severe back pain during her menstrual cycle to the list of substantial symptoms.

The endometriosis diet was also more restrictive: alcohol, caffeine, red meat, dairy, white carbs, white sugar, and soy. She hadn't been eating anything she enjoyed for quite a while.

Since half of our team was avoiding one thing or the other at the grocery store, it was difficult for us to put together meals with selective options. Leah wanted freedom. She told us during one of the meals in El Salvador that she felt God was going to heal her during this journey. We all looked at each other, not knowing how to respond. Although nobody said it, some of us certainly thought this was crazy.

We wished her well with that and went on about our business.

She had not been healed by the end of July. Her symptoms had remained consistent through the Race. This seeming lack of response to her prayer was disheartening. She questioned her faith and at times felt it had been lost completely. Leah and I were put on different teams for the last five months of the Race. When I saw her again near the end of our time in Chile, I noticed her eating ice cream. I asked her if she was just willing to suffer the symptoms for the taste.

"What? Oh, no. Haven't you heard? I'm healed," she stated, nonchalantly.

"You can eat ice cream now?" I asked.

"All the things," she replied.

"Yeah, Leah can eat anything now," her teammate, Kelly, told me as she chimed into our conversation.

The two of them started naming off things she had previously had allergic reactions to. They said she had decided to start testing them out. She continued this through Argentina.

The true test came at the end of our final month together. She had been trying the foods that cause reactions to endometriosis and her cycle was coming. Her cycle came and went without incident during our final travel days home.

I never saw Leah worry about what she was eating again.

Leah had the faith to ask for a miracle. She asked with confidence even though it was hard and she asked without pretense. She made her request simply for its own sake and put her trust in her Father in Heaven. She told us during the first conversation in El Salvador that it might be crazy, but she could ask for anything.

We went grocery shopping together one last time in Georgia at a follow-up debrief six weeks after the Race concluded. Leah was sure we had plenty of ice cream.

Maybe that's the kind of crazy that can bring healing to us all.

PATRICK BOOTH

Thank You

Thank you all so much for your support, encouragement, and donations throughout this journey! This year has been an incredible experience. If I had a thousand pages to write in, I could not fully explain the amounts of faith, hope, and love that were inspired my fellow volunteers, the communities we served, and in myself. It would not be possible without your compassion for communities in need around the world!

I want to send a special thank you to all of my monthly donors. You all have been the backbone of a journey that is changing my life and opening a door to change lives in countless communities around the world!

PATRICK BOOTH CHARITIES

Throughout this journey, I have been blessed to experience community beyond borders and a sense of unity that reaches beyond personal prejudices. With this in mind, I have started a foundation to continue supporting a communal spirit that is focused on meeting simple basic needs and caring for one another.

www.patrickbooth.org

Our first initiative was to provide medical expenses for Hannah Grace, support other World Racers who desire to continue serving the world community, and provide a cornerstone for future volunteer opportunities.

I invite you to continue supporting the world community by providing a one-time donation or becoming a monthly partner with Patrick Booth Charities at the website listed above. Thank you!

PATRICK BOOTH

World Race Contacts

EL SALVADOR
Iglesia Gran Comisión
Calle el litoral # 5, Playa Las Flores
Puerto de La Libertad
La Libertad-El Salvador
english.igcla.com/cpn/la-libertad
+503 2346-2082

GUATEMALA
GO! Ministries
439 Westwood SC PMB 138
Fayetteville, NC 28314
www.goministries.info

HONDURAS
Centro Cristiano Encuentro
www.ccencuentro.org
+504 9912-0960

NICARAGUA
REAP Granada
8107 Sidlaw hills terrace
Chesterfield, VA 23838
www.REAPGranada.com
469-264-6162

PANAMA
Ken and Elena Orozco
YWAM New Cultures in East Panama
www.construyendoesperanza.weebly.com
Email: orozcofamily@gmail.com

MALAWI
Extending Hope
www.extendinghope.org

COLOMBIA
Fundacion Cuidad Refugio
Carrera 48 N° 65-94
Medellin, Antioquia-Colombia
www.ciudadrefugio.org
+57 4580-5858

ECUADOR
Pan de Vida
103 Winthrope Way
Jacksonville, NC 28540
www.pandevida.ec/v2
910-795-4988

PERU
IncaLink
PO Box 1321
Boone, NC 28607
www.incalink.org

BOLIVIA
Clovis and Lisette Guardia
Ricardo Muller- Casa Pastora
Barrio Miraflores
Roboré, Bolivia
ugaguede@yahoo.com.ar

CHILE
Misión Comunidad Bautista
Ignacio Carrera Pinto 1448
Barrio La Concepción
Los Andes, Chile
+9 6898-3296

ARGENTINA
Adulam
Street Monteagudo 2552
Pontevedra-CP 1761-Party Merlo
Buenos Aires-Argentina
+054 011-15-4022-2960

Treehouse Hostel
Phone#: +54 926-0453-9421
Facebook/Treehouse hostel

Marcelo Gustavo Becerra
Phone: +54 926-1327-2000
Email: marcelobecerra3@hotmail.com

PATRICK BOOTH

ABOUT THE AUTHOR

Patrick Booth continues to answer the calling to help and serve others. He is the founder of Patrick Booth Charities, a registered 501(c)3 that focuses on supporting struggling communities overseas. Additionally, Patrick Booth seeks to further his own mission opportunities through independent volunteer work with a wide variety of secular and Christian service organizations. He continues to share growth through his blog and seeks to keep communication strong with the international service community through social media.

Find him online:

boothabroad.wordpress.com
facebook.com/patrickboothcharities
instagram.com/patrickboothlcdc
pinterest.com/patrick_booth
twitter: @boothcharities

Made in the USA
San Bernardino, CA
30 March 2016